THINKING/WRITING

An Introduction to the Writing
Process for Students of English
as a Second Language

THINKING/WRITING

An Introduction to the Writing Process for Students of English as a Second Language

Martha Kilgore Rice/Jane Unaiki Burns
San Joaquin Delta College

Prentice-Hall, Inc., Englewood Cliffs, New Jersey 07632

Editorial/production supervision and
   interior design by *Andy Roney and Lisa Halttunen*
Cover design and illustrations © 1984 by *William Kobus*
Manufacturing buyer: *Harry P. Baisley*

Printed in the United States of America

10 9 8 7 6 5 4 3 2 1

0-13-918244-6   01

PRENTICE-HALL INTERNATIONAL (UK) LIMITED, *London*
PRENTICE-HALL OF AUSTRALIA PTY. LIMITED, *Sydney*
PRENTICE-HALL CANADA INC., *Toronto*
PRENTICE-HALL HISPANOAMERICANA, S.A., *Mexico*
PRENTICE-HALL OF INDIA PRIVATE LIMITED, *New Delhi*
PRENTICE-HALL OF JAPAN, INC., *Tokyo*
PRENTICE-HALL OF SOUTHEAST ASIA PTE. LTD., *Singapore*
EDITORA PRENTICE-HALL DO BRASIL, LTDA., *Rio de Janeiro*
WHITEHALL BOOKS LIMITED, *Wellington, New Zealand*

CONTENTS

Two **WRITING DESCRIPTIVE PARAGRAPHS** **15**

Exercises

Three   CLASSIFICATION   41

**Four   DESCRIBING BY TELLING FUNCTION
         OF PARTS   57**

Five   EXPLAINING PROCESS   83

Exercises

Six   COMPARING AND CONTRASTING   103

Exercises

Seven   USING EXAMPLES TO SUPPORT OR EXPLAIN   **139**

Exercises

Eight   **USING REASONS TO SUPPORT YOUR OPINION**   **155**

Exercises

PREFACE

GOALS OF THE BOOK

In this book we are working toward several goals. We would like our students to be able to understand and work through the thought processes necessary to achieve unity and coherence in a written paragraph. We want them to have a knowledge of the common words and phrases used as signals in well-structured paragraphs. We want them to have the vocabulary that is appropriate for the kinds of paragraphs which are introduced.

The book presents paragraph assignments which stress descriptive detail, classification, analysis and function, process, comparison and contrast, example, and reason. The "Guided Imagery" sections provide an opportunity for teacher-directed writing; these sections are explained in the teacher's guide.

BASIS FOR THE BOOK

The book developed out of what we viewed as a need for our ESL students to understand the concept of linearity, which is an integral part of paragraph and essay development in English. Because our students come from varied educational backgrounds and because the linear form of development is not common to all cultures,[1] we have offered simple guidelines for organizing information and ideas.

We assume that our students have valuable knowledge to communicate. We also know that they are hindered in communicating this knowledge by limited vocabularies and by unfamiliarity with the rhetorical forms of English expository prose. As a basis for this book, we have followed, on a simple level, the hierarchy of skills set out in Bloom's *Taxonomy of Educational Objectives,* stressing ". . . mental processes of organizing and reorganizing material to achieve a particular purpose."[2]

The book is aimed at students on the low intermediate level. The content material is information about the world around us—plants, animals, society, emotions.

We have not used models because we feel that unless students think through the material actively, they will not master it. Writing is an active process, a thinking process. We do not believe it can be taught by modeling alone—although there are merits to be found in modeling—and therefore we offer the process as a challenge to students to use what they know about the world and the English language to construct their ideas and to fit them into a pattern which is easily understood by the reader.

MARTHA K. RICE
JANE U. BURNS

---

[1]Robert B. Kaplan, "Cultural Thought Patterns in Inter-cultural Education," *Language Learning,* XVI, nos. 1 and 2 (1966), 1–20.

[2]Benjamin S. Bloom et al., *Taxonomy of Education Objectives, Handbook I: Cognitive Domain* (New York: David McKay Company, Inc., 1956), p. 204.

THINKING/WRITING

An Introduction to the Writing Process for Students of English as a Second Language

One

THE PARAGRAPH AS A WHOLE UNIT

The purpose of this workbook is to give you information which will help you to *organize* your writing more effectively.

The book is divided into eight chapters. You will practice different ways of organizing material—either information which you already have or information which you will be given—into paragraphs which will be easily understood. You will be asked to list information based on what you see around you, to explain how to do things, to express opinions and give reasons, to compare and contrast items, and to analyze structures and processes.

You will learn *key words and phrases* which will help you to write more clearly, and you will practice putting these key words and phrases in the right places in paragraphs. Most of all, you will be asked to think—to use your own abilities to reason and to draw conclusions and put them into written form.

PARTS OF THE PARAGRAPH

A paragraph has a very clear-cut structure. It has three major parts. The first part of the paragraph is called the *topic sentence*. It *introduces* the reader to the main idea of the paragraph. The second part of the paragraph is called the *body*. The body is made up of several sentences which *support, prove,* or *explain* the statement made in the topic sentence. The third part of the paragraph is called the *concluding sentence*. This sentence *summarizes* what has been said. If a paragraph contains all these parts, it will be well structured.

Starting with Sentences

EXERCISE 1-1. KEY WORDS AND PHRASES.   The key words which describe the functions of the parts of a paragraph have been used in the following sentences. Read each sentence to help you understand the meaning of the italicized word. Then write a sentence of your own using the word.

1. *introduce:* Mr. Smith had never met Mr. Jones. His friend *introduced* them.

   Your sentence: _____

   _____

2. *support:* The legs of the table *support* the top.

   Your sentence: _____

   _____

3. *prove:* When you subtract two numbers, you can *prove* your answer by adding.

   Your sentence: _____

   _____

4. *explain:* I will *explain* to you how to get to Main Street from here.

   Your sentence: _____

   _____

5. *summarize:* The reporter *summarized* the senator's long speech in three sentences.

   Your sentence: _____

   _____

Building a Paragraph

EXERCISE 1-2. COMPLETING A PARAGRAPH.   Fill in the necessary words or phrases in the following paragraph to make it complete.

A paragraph has _____ major parts. The _____ introduces the _____. The _____ supports, _____, or _____ the topic sentence. The _____ summarizes the _____. These are the major _____ of a paragraph.

Note: By completing these sentences, you have made a paragraph. It has a topic sentence, a body, and a conclusion. The first line is *indented*. This means that the first line is moved in a few spaces. All paragraphs should look like this:

Which sentence in the preceding paragraph is the topic sentence? _____

Which sentences are part of the body? _____

Which sentence is the concluding sentence? _____

THE TOPIC SENTENCE

A topic sentence introduces the *main idea* of the paragraph. It must do *two* things. *The first thing* a topic sentence must do is to *tell the general topic* which will be discussed in the paragraph. *The second thing* the topic sentence must do is to *tell the reader what kinds of things will be said about the topic*. For instance, I want to write a paragraph about my school. School is a large topic, however. In order to write a paragraph about it, I need to choose one aspect (part) to write about. I am then *limiting* my topic. If I decide to write a description of the school building, my topic sentence will be something like this:

The building in which I go to school is very large and very beautiful.

My reader will know from my topic sentence that my paragraph will give details which show the ways in which my school is large and beautiful.

Starting with Sentences

EXERCISE 1-3. TOPIC SENTENCES. Following are some topic sentences which could be developed into paragraphs. Underline the part of the sentence that tells the topic, and circle the part of the sentence that limits the topic.

Example: A car has several moving parts.

1. If you want to bake a cake, you will have to follow several steps.

2. To become a draftsman, you must be able to do several things well.

3. The structures of plants have many similarities.

4. There are two major differences between men and women.

5. Before learning to swim, you must be able to do two things.

6. There are several steps in learning to swim.

7. Students who are good readers will do better in all their classes.

8. There are five steps which must be followed in writing a well-structured essay.

9. Several factors make democracy a good system of government.

10. Most well-structured compositions are divided into three parts.

EXERCISE 1-4. LIMITING THE TOPIC.   Following is a list of words taken from the sentences on page 5. They are general words which are often used to help *limit* the topic and point out the direction in which the paragraph will move. There is also a list of general topics which could be developed into paragraphs. Using both lists, practice writing topic sentences.

Example: General word: steps
Topic: changing a tire
Sentence: There are several steps in changing a tire.

GENERAL WORDS	TOPICS
steps	in making a dress
things	to do in studying for a test
differences	between boys and girls
similarities	between plants and animals
parts	in an engine

Begin each sentence with *There are.*

1. There are ⎯⎯⎯⎯⎯ steps in ⎯⎯⎯⎯⎯⎯⎯⎯⎯⎯⎯⎯⎯⎯⎯⎯⎯⎯⎯

2. ⎯⎯⎯⎯⎯⎯⎯⎯⎯⎯⎯⎯⎯⎯⎯⎯⎯⎯⎯⎯⎯⎯⎯⎯⎯⎯⎯⎯⎯⎯⎯⎯⎯⎯⎯⎯

3. ⎯⎯⎯⎯⎯⎯⎯⎯⎯⎯⎯⎯⎯⎯⎯⎯⎯⎯⎯⎯⎯⎯⎯⎯⎯⎯⎯⎯⎯⎯⎯⎯⎯⎯⎯⎯

4. ⎯⎯⎯⎯⎯⎯⎯⎯⎯⎯⎯⎯⎯⎯⎯⎯⎯⎯⎯⎯⎯⎯⎯⎯⎯⎯⎯⎯⎯⎯⎯⎯⎯⎯⎯⎯

5. ⎯⎯⎯⎯⎯⎯⎯⎯⎯⎯⎯⎯⎯⎯⎯⎯⎯⎯⎯⎯⎯⎯⎯⎯⎯⎯⎯⎯⎯⎯⎯⎯⎯⎯⎯⎯

6. ⎯⎯⎯⎯⎯⎯⎯⎯⎯⎯⎯⎯⎯⎯⎯⎯⎯⎯⎯⎯⎯⎯⎯⎯⎯⎯⎯⎯⎯⎯⎯⎯⎯⎯⎯⎯

Building a Paragraph

Note: If a sentence is a fact or if it is too specific, it will not make a good topic sentence. For instance, a simple statement such as the following would not be a good topic sentence.

Everyone will eventually die.

This is a fact and does not need to be proved. If the sentence had said instead *All humans pass through different stages from birth to death,* you could mention the fact that one of the stages is death, and you could also name the other stages.

EXERCISE 1-5. SELECTING A TOPIC SENTENCE.   Some of the following sentences would make better topic sentences than others. Put a *TS* in front of the sentences which would make good topic sentences. Put an *F* in front of the sentences which would not.

_____ 1. An elephant's trunk is used in many ways.

_____ 2. An elephant's trunk is very long.

_____ 3. The crepe myrtle tree produces beautiful pink blossoms in the fall.

_____ 4. There are many trees which produce beautiful flowers.

_____ 5. *The Old Man and the Sea* is a novel written by Ernest Hemingway.

_____ 6. *The Old Man and the Sea* deals with several interesting ideas.

_____ 7. Learning English is difficult.

_____ 8. Learning English is difficult for several reasons.

THE BODY

You may *support* your topic sentence in a number of ways. You might choose to give *descriptive details* or *facts*. If I were to write a topic sentence like *The pineapple is a beautiful fruit,* I would prove this to you by describing what is beautiful about the fruit.

If I had a topic sentence like *A college education is important for success in life,* I would support the topic sentence by giving you reasons why I think a college education is important for success.

If I had a topic sentence like *There are many kinds of evergreen trees,* I would support the topic sentence by giving you examples of the many kinds of trees.

Starting with Sentences

EXERCISE 1-6.   SUPPORTING THE TOPIC SENTENCE.   Look at the following topic sentences and decide if you would support them by giving *reasons, examples, descriptive details*, and/or *facts*. Some of the sentences may be supported by using two methods. Underline the part(s) of the sentences which helped you to make your decision.

> **Example:**   I find studying for examinations in college very difficult for three reasons.   (reason)

1. Mr. Smith is one of the most unusual looking men I have ever seen.
   _____

2. There are many kinds of insects which have highly structured societies._____

3. Smoking is considered to be dangerous to good health for several reasons._____

4. If I were going to construct a house, I would have to complete several steps._____

5. You need to have mathematics skills in order to become an architect._____

6. A good mechanic understands some of the basic principles of car design._____

7. I believe that a perfect society would have to have certain basic elements._____

8. There are three things about soccer which make it an exciting sport.
   _____

9. I like soccer for several reasons. _____

10. Dean McNulty was a very difficult man to get along with. _____

Building a Paragraph

It is important that all the information in a paragraph relates directly back to the topic sentence. If you put in details which are not necessary or are not about the topic, your reader will become bored and lost. If the details are directly related to the topic, they are *relevant*. If you include details which are not necessary, they are *irrelevant*.

EXERCISE 1-7.   RELEVANT DETAILS.   Read the following two paragraphs. They both describe the same thing, but one is better because all the information is *relevant*. Decide which paragraph is better. Then cross out the *irrelevant* information in the weaker paragraph.

1.   There are several things I must do to get my child ready for preschool. First, I have to give him a bath. I undress him while the water is running into the tub; then, when the tub is full, I wash him carefully. After his bath is finished, I dry him off with a towel and rub baby powder on him. Then I take him into the bedroom and dress him in the clothes which I have laid out for him to wear. When he is all dressed, I let him watch television for a few minutes while I get dressed. Then we leave for preschool.

2.   There are several things I must do to get my child ready for preschool. First, I give him a bath. He likes to play in the water and often makes a mess on the floor. Then I have to clean it up, and it takes me a long time. I wish he wouldn't do that, but it makes him happy. When he is finished with his bath, I dry him off with a towel and put some baby powder on him. The baby powder is kept on the third shelf of the closet, so I have to hold him and get the powder down at the same time. After that, I choose the clothes which he will wear. He has lots of clothes that his father and I have bought for him. His grandmother buys him clothes, too. On Easter last year, he got four new outfits. Next, I put the clothes on him. He always likes to watch television, so I let him do that before he goes to preschool each day. He likes "Sesame Street." These are the things I have to do to get my child ready for preschool.

THE CONCLUDING SENTENCE

A concluding sentence lets your reader know that the paragraph is finished. It summarizes what has been written in the paragraph. Some paragraphs do not need concluding sentences. In a descriptive paragraph, for example, if the writer has described the person or event or scene well enough in the body of the paragraph, there is no need to summarize for the reader. Paragraphs which are developed by reason or example, however, very often need concluding sentences.

Starting with Sentences

EXERCISE 1-8.   RECOGNIZING CONCLUDING SENTENCES.   The concluding sentence often contains the main ideas which have been mentioned in the paragraph. Study the last sentence in each paragraph and underline the ideas that have been restated.

1.   There were several reasons why Bob decided not to attend college this summer. To begin with, his ten-hour shift at the plant left little time for studying and listening to lectures. He couldn't afford to give up his job, as he had spent all his scholarship money. Then, his wife was pregnant with their third child and needed help with the children when he was at home. Thus college had to be postponed until his financial and personal situation improved.

How was this paragraph supported? Check one of the following blanks.

Reasons _____

Examples _____

2.   Travelers in the South and West Pacific should always be very careful of their health. For example, in the more remote areas one must take special precautions with food and water. Wash all uncooked food before eating and boil all drinking water. Other problems may be caused by bites from disease-carrying mosquitoes. These can cause malaria and dengue fever. Medication may be taken to prevent malaria, but there is nothing that can be taken to prevent dengue fever. One must try to avoid insect bites by using insect repellant, sleeping in screened rooms, and wearing long-sleeved shirts and pants. If these steps are taken, travelers should be able to avoid some of the health problems of the area.

How was this paragraph developed? Check one of the following spaces.

Reasons _____

Facts _____

Examples _____

Exercise 1-9. Writing Concluding Sentences. Read the following paragraphs and decide what information should be in the concluding sentences. Underline the words in the paragraph first to help you locate the ideas that you will restate. Part of the concluding sentences have been started for you.

1. Federal assistance for the victims of the Coalinga earthquake has been extended in several ways. For example, those homeowners with extensive damage to their homes may qualify for low-interest government loans. Others whose houses do not need major repairs may receive federal grants. Temporary housing has also been provided by means of federally owned trailers and private rental units paid for by the U.S. government. Thus earthquake victims

may receive _____,

_____, _____

_____.

How was this paragraph developed? Check one of the following spaces.

Reasons _____

Facts _____

Examples _____

2. Matt received an auto repair bill that annoyed him for several reasons. To begin with he hadn't received an estimate before work was done on the car, and the bill was much higher than he thought it would be. He saw that he had been charged full price for new parts instead of the sale price the garage was advertising in the newspaper. The labor costs were twice as high as they had been for his last repair job for the same work. Finally, the mechanic had put in an extra part that he had not wanted and charged him for the extra

labor. Matt was really angry that his bill was _____

_____

_____.

How was this paragraph developed? Check one of the following spaces.

Reasons _____

Facts _____

Examples _____

Building a Paragraph

EXERCISE 1-10. CHOOSING A CONCLUDING SENTENCE. Read the following paragraph and choose the best concluding sentence from the three listed. Copy the sentence on the last line.

    There are two possible advantages to be gained from knowing how to paraphrase. First, if you are able to translate what you read into your own words, you will find that you are reading more efficiently and, more important, remembering the material longer. Second, your college assignments often require you to read a journal article or a book and to write a report on what you have read. The more experience you have in paraphrasing, the easier it will be

for you to write reports. (concluding sentence) _____

_____

_____

1. Knowing how to paraphrase enables you to be more effective in both reading and writing.

2. Knowing how to paraphrase will give you two advantages.

3. College assignments often require you to write reports.

GUIDED IMAGERY

_____

_____

_____

_____

_____

_____

_____

_____

_____

_____

_____

_____

_____

_____

_____

_____

_____

_____

_____

_____

_____

_____

_____

_____

_____

_____

_____

EXERCISE 1-11. CHECKING UP. Answer the following questions.

1. A paragraph should be indented. Draw a picture which shows what *indent* means.

2. What does the topic sentence do? _____

    _____

3. If a paragraph contains information which is *not necessary,* this informa- tion is *irrelevant.* If irrelevant means not necessary, *what does relevant information mean?*

    _____

4. Which sentence in a paragraph *summarizes* the paragraph?

    _____

5. How many parts are there in a paragraph? (Circle the correct number.)
         one   two   three   four

Fill in the blanks on the following chart. The first one has been done for you.

Part	Function
topic sentence	introduces the topic
body	_____
concluding sentence	_____

Two

WRITING DESCRIPTIVE PARAGRAPHS

In this chapter you will be doing some pre-exercises which should help you decide what kinds of information you might want to put into a simple descriptive paragraph. It is necessary to observe closely the object or area which you are describing *and to see things in terms of their size, shape, and texture, or physical appearance.* It is also sometimes necessary to take into consideration all the separate parts of the total picture and describe them *in relationship to each other.*

Key words and phrases are used in some descriptive paragraphs because they indicate the location of one object or part in relationship to another object or whole. You will practice using a few of the more common key words of location in your own writing. This kind of descriptive detail is important for the writing assignments you may be asked to do in college or on the job.

You will be writing paragraphs which describe single objects and persons, rooms, and arrangements of objects.

PRE-EXERCISE 2-A. SEEING SIMILARITIES AND DIFFERENCES. Write a short sentence, following the pattern of sentence 1, which explains your choice for each of the items in the figure.

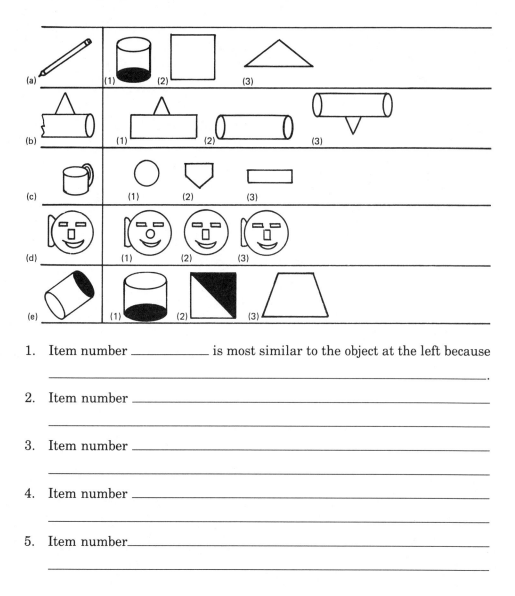

1. Item number _____ is most similar to the object at the left because

    _____.

2. Item number _____

    _____

3. Item number _____

    _____

4. Item number _____

    _____

5. Item number_____

    _____

PRE-EXERCISE 2-B.   SEEING SIMILARITIES AND DIFFERENCES.   Look at the shape or object in the box at the left. Find the shape at the right which you feel is most similar and circle it.

1. Item number ——————— is most similar to the object at the left because

    ———.

2. Item number ———

    ———

3. Item number ———

    ———

4. Item number ———

    ———

5. Item number———

    ———

ADJECTIVE ORDER AND PLACEMENT

When you use more than one word (adjective) to describe a noun, you usually follow a pattern for placement of the adjectives.

The word closest to the noun will be the adjective which defines it. Words which define *color* (*red, blue, green*) or *material* (*wooden, plastic*) are usually placed next to the noun when you are using more than one adjective.

	A–1	A–2

Examples: She was a *little yellow* chicken.

	A–1	A–2

He had a *large blue* car.

	A–1	A–2

He sat on a *red plastic* chair.

If you are using more than two adjectives, you should follow the preceding rule for the adjective which comes closest to the noun. The following diagram shows the position of other kinds of adjectives.

SIZE ——→	SHAPE ———→	COLOR ——→	MATERIAL
tiny	round	red	plastic
huge	square	blue	woolen
large	circular	yellow	wooden
small	triangular	green	brick

Note: You should try to avoid using more than two or three adjectives together as modifiers of one noun.

EXERCISE 2-1.   ADJECTIVE ORDER.   Rearrange the adjectives below so that they are in the correct order.

Example: round   large   bottle
<u>large   round   bottle</u>

1. brick   red   tiny   house

2. flower-covered   stone   wall

3. velvet   big   blue   couch

4. plastic   round   small   table

5. rectangular   long   silver   object

6. red   large   round   box

7. wooden   small   square   container

8. blue   denim   jeans

9. red   woolen   jacket

10. small   plastic   black   chair

Starting with Sentences

We use adjectives to help our readers see as clearly as possible the nouns we are describing. Keep your word order simple and place the adjectives as close as possible to the nouns which they are modifying. There are several ways of doing this in English. Two positions for adjective placement follow.

Position 1: The adjective is placed in front of the noun.

ADJ.   NOUN

Example: The *little old* man walked slowly into the *broken-down old* house.

Explanation: *Little* and *old* are two adjectives which describe the *man*. *Broken-down* and *old* are two adjectives which describe the *house*. They have been placed directly in front of the nouns that they modify.

Position 2: The adjective is placed after the verb if the verb is a *state-of-being* verb. These verbs do not show action. The most common state-of-being verbs are the forms of the verb *to be: is, are, was, were, will be, has been, had been, will have been.* The verbs *to smell, to taste, to feel, to become, to look,* and *to appear* can also be state-of-being verbs.

NOUN   STATE-OF-BEING VERB   ADJ.

Example: The old man was *little*

Explanation: *Little* still modifies the *man,* but it follows the past tense of the verb *to be.*

EXERCISE 2-2.   ADJECTIVE PLACEMENT.   Practice placing adjectives in the two positions just given. Use a form of the verb *to be.*

NOUN   ADJ.

Example: the dog   big, black

Position 1: the big black dog

Position 2: The dog was big and black.

NOUN   ADJ.

1. the window   open

Position 1: _____

Position 2: _____

NOUN   ADJ.

2. the building   large, square

Position 1: _____

Position 2: _____

NOUN   ADJ.

3. the man   handsome

Position 1: _____

Position 2: _____

Note: Look back at the answers you have written. By using position 2, you have created a complete sentence. By using position 1, you have not completed a sentence. You must add more to the group of words in position 1 in order to make a complete sentence.

Look at the following example and explanation and then the practice exercise on adding more information to a sentence.

If you want to express something about the *awful food* you have eaten for dinner, you might write a sentence by using the adjective and noun in position 1.

Example: *The awful food* made me ill.

If you choose to use position 2—*The food was awful*—you will have to find another way to express the fact that *it made you ill.*

Examples: The food was awful, and it made me ill.
The food was awful. It made me ill.

Explanation: In the first example the two ideas have been expressed in a *compound* sentence. That is, two complete sentences have been joined together by the comma and the conjunction *and*. In the second example, the new information has been added in a new sentence. A period has been placed between the two sentences, and the first word in the second sentence, *It,* has been capitalized.

EXERCISE 2-3.   PLACING ADJECTIVES.   Practice placing the adjectives in the two positions. Then follow the directions for adding more information to the sentences.

                NOUN   ADJ.

Example: grandmother patient

Position 1: The patient grandmother _____

Position 2: The grandmother was patient. _____

Tell what she did.

Position 1: The patient grandmother was not upset by the children.

Position 2: The grandmother was patient, and she was not upset by the children.

or: The grandmother was patient. She was not upset by the children.

     NOUN   ADJ.

1. the woman beautiful young

Position 1: _____

Position 2: _____

Tell what she did.

Position 1: _____

Position 2: _____

_____

or: _____

_____

     NOUN   ADJ.

2. the chair dark brown

Position 1: _____

Position 2: _____

_____

Tell where it was located.

Position 1: _____

Position 2: _____

_____

or: _____

_____

NOUN   ADJ.

3. the man   handsome

Position 1: _____

Position 2: _____

_____

Tell what he did.

Position 1: _____

Position 2: _____

_____

or: _____

_____

WRITING A TOPIC SENTENCE

Topic sentences for descriptive paragraphs often mention *general characteristics* which need to be supported with clear details.

A topic sentence for a paragraph describing an *ugly old woman* might be something like this:

The *old* woman was *ugly*.

Here *old* and *ugly* are the words which limit the topic of *woman*. Since they are general adjectives, you can supply details which will make them clearer.

Here are some details which might support this topic sentence.

1. She was bent over.
2. She had stringy gray hair.
3. She wore ragged clothing.
4. She was very skinny.
5. Her nose was long and pointed.
6. She walked with a limp.

These details "prove" that the old woman was ugly. If you put them into paragraph form, they might read like this:

The old woman was ugly. She was bent over and walked with a limp. Her nose was long and pointed, and her hair was gray and stringy. Her clothes were ragged, and they hung loosely on her skinny body.

Starting with Sentences

EXERCISE 2-4.   WRITING TOPIC SENTENCES.   Practice writing topic sentences for the following topics. Look back at the example if you need help.

> **Example:**   a large, crowded auditorium
>
> The large auditorium was crowded.
>
> or The crowded auditorium was large
>
> or The auditorium was large and crowded.

1. the frightened little boy

   _____

2. the broken-down old house

   _____

3. the shiny new car

   _____

4. the freshly painted room

   _____

5. the beautiful spring flowers

   _____

6. the dirty kitchen

   _____

7. the triumphant tired runner

   _____

8. the dying tree

   _____

9. the small crowded room

   _____

EXERCISE 2-5.   MATCHING DETAILS WITH TOPICS.   Match the details below with the correct topics. Write them on the lines where they fit. Use the topic sentences which you wrote in the exercise on page 25 for the first sentence.

1.   The shingles were off the roof.

2.   The paint had no scratches on it.

3.   He hid behind his mother's skirts.

4.   The door was off its hinges.

5.   The inside smelled like new leather.

6.   The windows were broken.

7.   His eyes were filled with tears.

8.   He was shaking.

9.   The chimney bricks were crumbling.

10.   The sun reflected off the clean windshield.

Topic: the shiny car

Your topic sentence: _____

Details: _____

_____

_____

_____

_____

_____

_____

Topic: the frightened little boy

Your topic sentence: _____

Details: _____

_____

_____

_____

_____

Topic: the broken-down old house

Your topic sentence: _____

Details: _____

_____

_____

_____

_____

_____

Building a Paragraph

EXERCISE 2-6.   DESCRIBING AN OBJECT.   Look carefully at the preceding object. Fill in the blanks with information which would help you describe it.

1.   Number of parts: _____

_____

2.   Shape of parts: _____

_____

3.   Size of parts: _____

_____

4.   Location of parts: _____

EXERCISE 2-7.   DESCRIBING NUMBER AND SHAPE.   Write a topic sentence by filling in the blanks with information about the number of parts and the shapes of the parts.

The object is made up of (number)   (shape) .

EXERCISE 2-8.   DESCRIBING SIZE AND LOCATION.   Now fill in the blanks with information which tells about the *size* and *location* of the shapes. Write the topic sentence on the first line.

(Topic sentence) _____ .

A _____ is located _____. There are _____

small diamond shapes attached to the _____ at the four _____ .

The object looks like _____ .

EXERCISE 2-9.   DESCRIBING A PERSON.   Look around the room and find a person whom you would like to describe. Do not write about the person's personality. Describe the person only in terms of his or her physical characteristics. Make notes on the following blanks before writing your paragraph. Be sure that you have a topic sentence. (The teacher may want to vary this exercise by bringing in photographs of people for the students to describe.)

Height: _____

Weight: _____

Hair (color, length, texture): _____

Skin (color, texture): _____

Facial features (nose, mouth, eyes): _____

Clothes (color, style): _____

_____

Topic sentence: Fill in the blanks with two adjectives that describe the person you have chosen.

The _____ (person) was _____.

_____

_____

_____

_____

_____

_____

_____

_____

_____

_____

_____

_____

_____

_____

_____

SPATIAL RELATIONSHIPS

Another way of describing something is by locating it in space in relationship to something else. To express this spatial relationship—that is, the location of an object or objects in terms of familiar key words and phrases—study the following list.

to the right of
The circle is located to the right of the square.
on the right side of, on the right of
The circle is located on the right side of the square.

to the left of
The house is located to the left
of the grocery store.

next to
The chair is next to the table.
adjacent to
The chair is adjacent to the table.

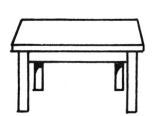 

in front of
The boy is in front of the girl.

behind, in back of
The boy is standing behind the girl.
The boy is standing in back of the girl.

under
The hat is under the coat.
on top of
The ball is on top of the table.
in the middle of
The table is in the middle of the room.

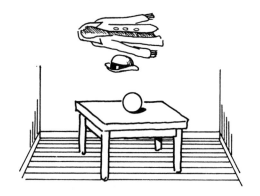

EXERCISE 2-10. DEFINING SPATIAL RELATIONSHIPS. Study the pictures and answer the questions.

1. What is the relationship of the shaded triangle in the picture at the right to the two triangles behind it?

_____

_____

2. List all the shapes adjacent to the circle in the picture.

_____

_____

3. Using one of the words or phrases from the list, tell the location of the triangle in relation to the circles.

_____

_____

4. Explain the location of the circle in relation to the first two triangles.

_____

_____

5a. In what section of the picture are the two triangles located?

_____

_____

5b. One circle is located mostly in the lower right-hand section. Where is the other circle located?

_____

_____

EXERCISE 2-11. DESCRIBING SPATIAL RELATIONSHIPS. Write as many sentences as you can describing the relationship between the following objects.

Example: The ball is on top of the square.
The square is under the ball.

1. _____
_____
_____

2. _____
_____
_____

3. _____
_____
_____

4. _____
_____
_____

5. _____
_____
_____

EXERCISE 2-12.   ORDERING DETAILS—THE GLOBE.   Study the picture carefully. Look at the objects and decide how you would describe them. Think of the adjectives that tell size and shape. Describe the location of the objects by using the key words and phrases. Write your notes about the objects in the following chart.

Object	Location	Description
globe	on top of the desk	round and blank; set on a triangular base

_____

_____

_____

_____

_____

_____

_____

_____

_____

_____

_____

_____

_____

ORDERING A DESCRIPTIVE PARAGRAPH

It is important to follow some kind of order in writing a descriptive paragraph. For example, in the preceding paragraph you began by describing the globe and then describing the other objects *in relation to* the globe. Sometimes you may want to imagine that you are in the picture and begin from whatever point you imagine yourself to be standing or sitting.

EXERCISE 2-13. WRITING A DESCRIPTIVE PARAGRAPH. A. Your teacher will read to you and have you imagine that you are in the place that is being described. When you are through listening to the teacher, draw what you saw in the following space.

B. Look at your drawing and remember some of the qualities of the things which are in the picture (texture, size, shape, color). Write a paragraph describing the scene. Start by describing the park bench and describe the other things by telling where they are located *in relation to* the park bench and then by *telling their qualities*. Be sure to give all the information about each object before you go on to the next.

1. The park bench is located _____ . It is

    _____

2. (trees) _____

    _____

3. (flowers) _____

    _____

4. (trash can) _____

_____

_____

_____

C. Write a topic sentence which will introduce your paragraph. Tell where the spot is located and generally describe what it looks like (general words might be *beautiful, neat, lovely,* and so on).

_____

_____

D. Put all your sentences together into paragraph form.

_____

_____

_____

_____

_____

_____

_____

_____

_____

_____

_____

_____

E. Think of a sentence which might summarize the place in the park. Put it on the end of the preceding paragraph. It will be your concluding sentence.

EXERCISE 2-14.   DESCRIBING A ROOM.   A. Your instructor will draw a diagram of a room on the board. He or she will tell you where to place the doors, windows, and furniture. Listen carefully and draw the objects in their correct places in the room on this page. Check your diagram with the one on the board.

B. Decide how you would describe the objects in the room. Use the adjectives that describe size, shape, color, texture, and material. Describe the location of the objects by using the key words and phrases. Write your notes about the objects in the following chart.

Object	Location	Description

C. *Topic sentence:* In your topic sentence make a statement about the size and shape of the room.

The room is _____

_____

D. *The body:* Complete the paragraph by writing sentences describing the objects in the room and their locations.

    Topic sentence _____

_____

Body _____

_____

_____

_____

_____

_____

_____

_____

_____

_____

_____

_____

_____

_____

EXERCISE 2-15.   CHECKING UP.   Answer the questions in your own words.

1.   What is a descriptive paragraph? _____

_____

2.   Information about the size, shape, and color of an object helps your reader understand the object which you are describing. (Circle one of the following answers.)
   a.   true
   b.   false

Use the following key words and phrases in sentences.

1.   adjacent to _____

_____

2.   to the right of _____

_____

3.   to the left of_____

_____

4.   on top of_____

_____

Three

CLASSIFICATION

In Chapter 2 we concentrated on describing things according to their physical characteristics. The paragraphs gave information about size, shape, color, texture, and location. Another way to describe something is to *classify* it. *Classifying things means that you put like things together in groups.* To help your reader understand why you have classified these particular items, you must define your groups. Then you must take one of the items (an object, an animal, a person, or an event) and describe it. This item is an example of the classified group.

There are several "thinking" steps which you will take as you write your paragraph. For instance, if you were going to write about bottom-feeding fish and sea creatures, you might ask yourself the following questions:

1. What are the kinds of animals that live on the bottom of the sea?
2. Are they all fish, or are some of them other kinds of creatures?
3. How are they alike?
4. How are they different?
5. How can I classify them?
6. How can I label the lists?
7. What can I say in the topic sentence?
8. What information shall I put in the body of the paragraph?

Some key words and phrases are used in classifying and describing groups. You will practice using these in sentences and paragraphs.

In your paragraphs you will write about groups and categories of things and explain how they are classified.

PRE-EXERCISE 3-A: DEFINING, CLASSIFYING, LABELING. Definition: An insect has three specific characteristics—a segmented body, three pair of legs, and two pair of wings.
Study the pictures, find three animals that fit the definition, and write their names in the blank.

The _____, the _____, and the _____ are examples of insects.

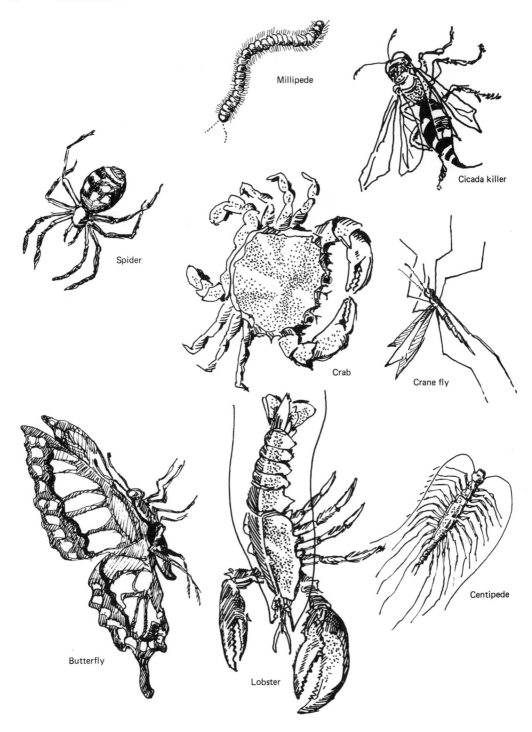

Millipede

Cicada killer

Spider

Crab

Crane fly

Butterfly

Lobster

Centipede

PRE-EXERCISE 3-B.   DEFINING, CLASSIFYING, LABELING.   Definition: There are various kinds of land formations. Some kinds are raised, sloping parts of the earth's surface, and some kinds are flat areas of land.
Study the diagram and find the formations that belong to the two groups. Write them in the blanks.

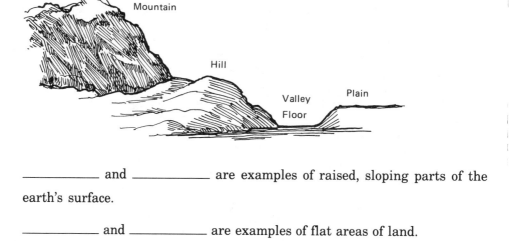

_____ and _____ are examples of raised, sloping parts of the earth's surface.

_____ and _____ are examples of flat areas of land.

PRE-EXERCISE 3-C.   DEFINING, CLASSIFYING, LABELING.   Definition: There are various kinds of bodies of water. Some kinds are completely enclosed by land and some kinds are open areas of sea water.
Study the diagram and find the formations that belong to the two groups. Write their names in the blanks.

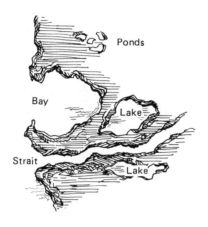

_____ and _____ are examples of bodies of water completely enclosed by land.

_____ and _____ are examples of open areas of sea water.

PRE-EXERCISE 3-D.   DEFINING, CLASSIFYING, LABELING.   Study the following list of items. They are all examples of kinds of land transportation. The items may be grouped together. *Write* their names in the blanks under Group 1 and Group 2. *Label* the groups.

bicycle   truck
unicycle   motorcycle
car   elephant
horse

GROUP 1: _____   **GROUP 2:** _____

_____   _____

_____   _____

_____

_____

_____

Divide Group 1 into two smaller groups. *Write* their names in the blanks. *Label* the groups.

GROUP 1a: _____   **GROUP 1b:** _____

_____   _____

_____   _____

_____

DEFINING KEY WORDS AND PHRASES IN YOUR OWN WORDS

Starting with Sentences

In order to write a description that uses examples to support and prove your topic sentence, you will be grouping things together and naming the group. Putting things into the group is called *classifying*. A group is called a *category*. Naming the group is called *labeling*.

EXERCISE 3-1. USING KEY WORDS AND PHRASES.   Write a sentence of your own, using the following words.

1. (category) _____

    _____

2. (classifying) _____

    _____

3. (labeling) _____

    _____

Things that belong together are called *kinds, types,* or *sorts.* A kind, a sort, or a type can be a person, a thing, or an event that represents the group.

> **Examples:**   *One kind of* bird is an eagle.
> Birthdays are *one type of* celebration.
> An FBI agent is *one sort of* government official.

Your sentence:

4. (kind) _____

    _____

5. (type) _____

    _____

6. (sort) _____

    _____

Another way of talking about a group is to use the word *variety.* A variety is a number of different things thought of as being together in a collection.

> **Example:**   There are several *varieties* of monkeys in the zoo.

7. (variety) _____

    _____

Something that is selected from the group to illustrate the character of the group is called an *example.*

> **Example:**   There are several kinds of animals in the primate family.
> *For example,* a monkey is a member of the family.

8. (for example) _____

_____

_____

An action that is characteristic of a group or parts of an animal or plant is called a *function*.

> **Example:**   The *function* of the heart is to pump blood through the body.

9. (function) _____

_____

WRITING A TOPIC SENTENCE

Several key words are useful in writing a topic sentence for a paragraph that uses examples. You have already reviewed these and practiced writing sentences of your own. Now you will see the words used in the topic sentence. Study these examples.

1. kinds: There are several kinds of prejudice.
2. varieties: There are several varieties of beans.
3. sorts: There are several sorts of people whom I like to be with.
4. examples: Several examples of prehistoric life were found at the site.
5. types: In any school you will find several different types of teachers.

These words indicate to your reader that you will be defining kinds, varieties, sorts, examples, or types of something and will be supporting your definition with descriptive detail and examples.

EXERCISE 3-2.   SELECTING A TOPIC SENTENCE.   Read the following sentences and underline them if you think they can be developed into paragraphs that would use examples to prove or support the topic sentence.

1. There are a variety of immigrants who have come to California to live.

2. My uncle has the largest pair of hands I have ever seen.

3. There are at least five kinds of nursery schools in town.

4. There are four dogs in my house.

5. Several examples of newly harvested fruit may be seen in the supermarket.

Starting with Sentences

EXERCISE 3-3.   ORDERING A PARAGRAPH.   This will be an oral in-class activity. The instructor will discuss the topic and the thinking steps before you begin to write.

1. Define your topic by deciding what the "limiter" in the topic sentence will be.
2. List all the items that you might consider writing about.
3. Decide if the items can be grouped according to similarities or differences.
4. Label the groups.
5. Take two or three of the items and use them as examples that prove or support your topic sentence.
6. Describe the examples and explain why you placed them into their groups.

Look at the following example.

> Most cars can be classified into one of three categories.

Step 1

What is the topic? _____

What is the paragraph going to tell you about the topic?

_____

Step 2

How would you define *kinds of cars?* To do this you might begin by making a list of the different kinds of cars you know.

_____

_____

_____

_____

_____

_____

Step 3

Look at the list and place the cars with similar characteristics together in the following columns. Think of such things as speed, size, comfort, and gas mileage.

	GROUP 1	*GROUP 2*	*GROUP 3*
Label	_____	_____	_____
	_____	_____	_____
	_____	_____	_____
	_____	_____	_____

Label the columns by grouping the cars into three classes: economy, luxury, and sports cars.

Step 4

Look at the following chart. On line *a* write in how fast you think the cars in the groups could go. On line *b* write in how big you think the cars are. On line *c* write in how many miles per gallon of gasoline you think the cars would get. On line *d* write in how comfortable you think the cars are. Would they have standard or deluxe features?

	Economy Cars	Luxury Cars	Sports Cars
a. *Speed*			
b. *Size*			
c. *Gas mpg*			
d. *Comfort*			

Write the definition of the three groups by choosing the correct word to complete the sentences. Circle the word.

An economy car gets more than (10, 20, 30) miles to the gallon. It is usually (small, medium, large) in size with (standard, deluxe) features. The top speed is about (80, 100, 120) miles per hour.

Complete the following sentences yourself.

A luxury car gets _____

_____

_____

_____

A sports car gets _____

_____

_____

_____

Step 5

Write the topic sentence. _____

_____

Write the definition of an economy car. _____

_____

_____

Take one example from the list of cars in Step 3 and tell why it fits in the group. Describe the car's speed, gas mileage, and size. Tell how comfortable you think the car is.

_____

_____

_____

Write the definition of a luxury car. _____

_____

_____

Take one example from the list of cars in Step 3 and tell why it fits in the group. Describe the car's speed, gas mileage, size, and degree of comfort.

_____

_____

_____

Write the definition of a sports car. _____

_____

_____

_____

Take one example from the list of cars in Step 3 and tell why it fits in the group. Describe the car's speed, gas mileage, size, and degree of comfort.

_____

_____

Building a Paragraph

GUIDED IMAGERY.

_____

_____

_____

_____

_____

_____

_____

_____

_____

_____

_____

_____

_____

_____

_____

_____

_____

_____

_____

_____

_____

_____

_____

_____

_____

_____

EXERCISE 3-4.   CONSUMER GOODS.   After the teacher discusses the topic of consumer goods with the class and introduces the idea of necessities and luxuries, you will be writing a paragraph about consumer goods. You will classify these into two groups and describe each group.

Step 1

List all the kinds of consumer goods you can think of.

_____

_____

_____

_____

_____

_____

_____

_____

Step 2

Write your topic sentence by filling in the blanks.

Consumer _____ may be _____ into two _____: necessities and luxuries.

Step 3

Group the items by deciding what qualities and characteristics the things have in common. Think about which things are necessary and useful and which things are used for pleasure. Label the groups.

GROUP 1: _____   *GROUP 2:* _____

_____   _____

_____   _____

_____   _____

_____   _____

_____   _____

Step 4

Describe the characteristics of each group by filling in the blanks in the following sentences.

Necessities are things that are _____ in our daily lives. We could _____ live without them.

Luxuries are _____ important things that are used for _____. We could _____ without them.

Step 5

Write the topic sentence (look back at step 1).

Consumer goods may be _____

_____

Write the definition of Group 1 (look at step 4).

Necessities are things _____

_____

Take one example from Group 1 (look at step 3) and tell how it fits in the group.

For example, _____ is a necessity. It is used _____

_____

Take a second example from Group 1 and tell how it fits in the group.

_____

_____

Take a third example from Group 1 and tell how it fits in the group.

_____

_____

Write the definition of Group 2 (look at step 4).

Luxuries are _____

_____

Take one example from Group 2 (look at step 3) and tell how it fits in the group.

For example, _____ is a luxury. It _____

_____

Take a second example from Group 2 and tell how it fits in the group.

_____

_____

Take a third example from Group 2 and tell how it fits in the group.

_____

_____

Step 6

Put your paragraph together.

Topic sentence: _____

_____

Definition of Group 1: _____

_____

First example: _____

_____

Second example: _____

_____

Third example: _____

_____

Definition of Group 2: _____

_____

First example: _____

_____

Second example: _____

_____

Third example: _____

_____

EXERCISE 3-5. CHECKING UP.   Complete the sentences with the correct words. Choose the words from the following vocabulary.

    kinds   label
    variety   example
    classify   categories

1. The teacher asked us to _____ the objects according to their similarities.

2. We were then asked to _____ each group with a name.

3. The _____ included a _____ of things.

4. From the two categories, we then had to choose an _____ which would best illustrate the group.

5. I did mine very well because I chose the right _____ of examples.

Four

DESCRIBING BY TELLING FUNCTION OF PARTS

Another way to describe something is to tell its *function. Function indicates an object's or person's use or purpose as a part of a structure.* For instance, if you were to describe the heart, you might describe it as an organ which is shaped like an irregular triangle and is located on the left side of the chest. You might also describe its function: It supplies oxygen to the other parts of the body by pumping blood through the system.

When you describe something by function, you may also give information about what it looks like or where it is located. How much you tell about the thing you're describing depends on the kind of information available.

In this chapter you will be doing exercises on classifying and labeling. *Classifying* means that you put like things together in groups. *Labeling* means that you name them by whatever they have in common.

You will also write paragraphs describing parts of a whole in terms of their function, location, and/or physical appearance.

The key words you will study are general verbs frequently used to describe *function* and often used to *limit topic sentences* for descriptive paragraphs of this sort.

PRE-EXERCISE 4-A. CLASSIFYING. The following items can be put into groups according to their use or function. Putting things which have similarities together is called *classifying.* Classifying things is a way of organizing them. Each group has been *labeled* for you. Put the items into the correct groups. Cross out any words which do not fit into the groups.

ammonia	hamburger	wood	cement
hammer	detergent	screws	electric saw
bricks	tomato soup	screwdriver	tea
oven cleaner	furniture polish	napkins	water

CLEANING SUPPLIES   **TOOLS**   **BUILDING MATERIALS**

_____   _____   _____

_____   _____   _____

_____   _____   _____

_____   _____   _____

_____   _____

PRE-EXERCISE 4-B.   CLASSIFYING.   Look carefully at the following words. They are all examples of vehicles. Some of the words may be grouped together. Find the words that you think have something in common and group them under the following headings.

ambulance	oil truck	mail truck	Salvation Army truck
police car	fire truck	moving van	bookmobile
cattle truck	UPS truck	bus	tow truck
dry-cleaning van			

VEHICLES

Vehicles used in emergencies:

_____

_____

_____

_____

Vehicles that transport people and
   animals:

_____

_____

Vehicles that make pickups and
   deliveries:

_____

_____

_____

_____

Vehicles that move out of state:

_____

_____

PRE-EXERCISE 4-C.   CLASSIFYING.   Look carefully at the following words. They are all buildings. Some of the words may be grouped together. Find the words that you think have something in common and group them under the headings given below.

disco	apartment	house	soccer field
condo	bookstore	movie theater	butcher shop
bakery	drugstore	hospital	duplex
theater	ice rink		

BUILDINGS

Buildings people live in:	Buildings people shop in:	Buildings people are entertained in:
_____	_____	_____
_____	_____	_____
_____	_____	_____
_____	_____	_____
_____	_____	_____

KEY WORDS AND PHRASES—VERBS

Starting with Sentences

EXERCISE 4-1.   USING VERBS.   A. Following are verbs commonly used to describe function. Look at the pictures and at the words. Then write sentences, using the verbs.

1. permits
    allows
    The window permits light to enter
      the room.

    _____ allows _____

    _____

2. supports

    _____ supports _____

    _____

3. protects

protects
_____

_____

4. manufactures

manufactures
_____

_____

B. Choose one of the words from the list for each sentence. Some of them are singular and some are plural. Be sure to choose the correct form.

    permit
    allow
    protects
    support
    manufacture

1. Windows _____ air to enter a room.

2. Clothing _____ our bodies from extreme cold.

3. Your facts don't _____ your opinion.

4. Don't _____ your children to swim alone.

5. Green leaves _____ food for plants.

THE TOPIC SENTENCE

Starting with Sentences

In Chapter 1 you were introduced to the idea of the topic sentence. This sentence tells about the main topic of the paragraph; it also tells the reader what kinds of things will be said about the topic. When you are writing about the functions of parts of things, the topic sentence will include some key words. Some words may be used interchangeably. Study the following examples.

section part component	The machine was divided into three *sections/parts/components*.
portion share	The cake was divided into five *portions/shares*.
segment part	The insect's body consisted of three major *segments/parts*.

These words refer to parts of a whole. The paragraph would then be developed by writing sentences that describe what each part does—in other words, its function.

Your topic sentence also tells how many parts the system has. If you are not sure of the exact number of parts, some useful words follow:

several many	There are *several* important components in a stereo set. An automobile consists of *many* parts.

Some useful verbs used in telling how many parts are

is made up of
consists of
is divided into
has

EXERCISE 4-2.   WRITING TOPIC SENTENCES.   A. Following is a list of topic sentences that can be developed into paragraphs. Underline those sentences that would introduce a paragraph describing the functions of parts of a system or whole.

1.   All insects have jointed bodies divided into separate parts.

2.   She had a tiny blue flower in her hand.

3.   Butterflies have three main body parts: head, thorax, and abdomen.

4.   She cancelled the appointment for a good reason.

5.   An orchestra is made up of several sections.

6.   A wristwatch consists of several components.

7.   The fishing rod was divided into several sections.

B. Practice using the key words and phrases by completing the following sentences.

1.   The human body consists of _____ _____.

2.   A   chair   has   _____ _____: the   _____,
     the _____, and the _____.

3.   A flashlight is divided into _____ _____.

4.   There are _____ major _____ in a pencil.

Building a Paragraph

EXERCISE 4-3. THE CONTAINER. This is an in-class activity. Look at the diagram of a container. Follow your instructor's directions, and fill in the chart with the necessary information.

Study the following list of words. These are useful adjectives that you might like to use in your description.

grooved	smooth	transparent
ridged	rubber	circular
shiny	clear	cylindrical

	Part	Function	Description
1.			
2.			

Write a topic sentence for your paragraph.

The container has _____ parts.

C. Copy the topic sentence which you wrote and complete the paragraph using the information found on the chart. Write your paragraph. Do not forget to indent.

_____

_____

_____

_____

_____

_____

_____

_____

_____

_____

_____

_____

_____

EXERCISE 4-4.   THE TOOL.   A. Look at the diagram. It is a tool—a hoe. Fill in the chart naming the tool's parts, their functions, and a description of the parts. Then write a topic sentence for a paragraph describing a hoe.

Study the following list of words. These are useful verbs that you might like to use in your description.

to allow	to dig	to join
to permit	to attach	to hold
to scoop		

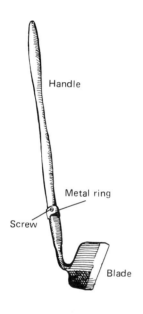

Handle

Metal ring

Screw

Blade

Part	Function	Description
1. Handle		
2. Blade		
3. Metal ring		
4. Screw		

Write a topic sentence for your paragraph.

The hoe _____.

B. Copy the topic sentence which you wrote and complete the paragraph using the information found on your chart. Write your paragraph. Do not forget to indent.

_____

_____

_____

_____

_____

_____

_____

_____

_____

_____

_____

_____

_____

_____

GUIDED IMAGERY

_____

_____

_____

_____

_____

_____

_____

_____

_____

_____

_____

_____

_____

_____

_____

_____

_____

_____

_____

_____

_____

_____

_____

_____

_____

_____

_____

_____

_____

_____

EXERCISE 4-5.   THE TREE.   A. The following chart names the parts of the tree and gives their functions. Fill in the column labeled "Location."

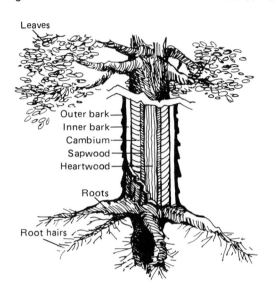

Leaves

Outer bark
Inner bark
Cambium
Sapwood
Heartwood

Roots

Root hairs

Part	Function	Location
1. leaves	manufacture food	on the branches
2. root hairs	take water and minerals from soil	
3. roots	support tree and carry water	
4. outer bark	protects tree	
5. inner bark	pathway by which food is carried to parts of tree	
6. cambium	parts of tree which allow growth and expansion	
7. heartwood	supports tree	
8. sapwood	carries water from roots to other parts of tree	

B.   Group the parts of the tree according to their common functions.

1.   List all the parts which manufacture food or take in and carry water in the column under "Nourishment."
2.   List all the parts which provide protection in another column.
3.   List all the parts which allow growth in another column.
4.   List all the parts which provide support in the last column.

Nourishment	Protection	Growth	Support

Note: Some of the columns should have more than one part of the tree listed. When you write your paragraph describing the parts of the tree, write about all the parts which provide nourishment; then write about all the parts which provide protection, growth, and support. This will give your paragraph a *logical order.*

C. Writing a topic sentence, body, and concluding sentence: A topic sentence which would introduce a paragraph describing the function of tree parts would most probably mention the word *parts*. It might also mention the major functions of the parts—*nourishment, protection, growth,* and *support.*
Using the verb *provide,* write a sentence which contains this information.

Topic sentence: The _____

provide _____

Supporting details: Write sentences describing the location and function of the parts of the tree.

The leaves, _____, _____, _____, and _____

provide nourishment by manufacturing food and carrying water and minerals

to the tree. Leaves are located _____and _____food.

Root hairs are located _____ and absorb _____ and _____.

The _____ are located underground and _____ water up to the

tree. The inner bark is _____ and is a pathway for

_____ to be carried to different parts of the tree. The sapwood is located

_____. It also carries _____. The outer bark is

_____ and provides protection. The cambium layer,

which is located next to the _____, allows the tree to _____. The

_____ and _____ give support to the _____. The heart-

wood is located _____, and the roots are located

_____.

Concluding sentence: Look back at the section on writing concluding sentences in
Chapter 1. Then choose the concluding sentence which you feel would be best.

1. The leaves are more important than any other parts of the tree.

2. Trees are beautiful.

3. All the parts depend on each other.

4. All the parts of a tree are important in maintaining its life and health.

ORDERING FACTS

What you write in your topic sentence should determine the order in
which things are mentioned in the paragraph. In the preceding exercise, the
topic sentence should have mentioned the four functions: *nourishment, protection, growth,* and *support.* Because nourishment was mentioned first in the
topic sentence, *it should have been explained first in the paragraph itself.* You
already know that it is important for your topic sentence to state clearly what
will follow in the paragraph. It is also important to make sure that if you
mention specific things in your topic sentence, you explain them in the same
order in the paragraph itself.

Starting with Sentences

EXERCISE 4-6.   ORDERING FACTS.   A. Read the following topic sentence carefully.

There are four main parts of a flowering plant: stem, roots, leaves, and flowers.

1.   What is the general topic? _____

2.   What is the limiting part of the sentence? _____

3.   What part of the flower will be mentioned first in the body of the paragraph? _____

4.   What part should be mentioned second? _____

5.   What part should be mentioned third? _____

6.   What part should be mentioned fourth? _____

B. Arrange the following sentences in the order in which you should find them in a paragraph which begins with this topic sentence. Number them 1, 2, 3, 4, and so on.

Topic sentence: There are four main parts of a flowering plant: stem, roots, leaves, and flowers.

_____   The stem is attached to the roots of the plant, which are underground.

_____   Central to the plant's life is the stem, a stalk which supports the flower and the leaves.

_____   The roots hold the plant in the ground and also store food.

_____   Besides the stem and the roots, there are two other major parts of the plant: the leaves and the flower.

_____ The stem has several purposes: It stores food, it manufactures some of the food, and it carries water to parts of the plant.

_____ Water is absorbed through the root hairs located at the ends of the roots and is carried up through the roots to the stem and then to the rest of the plant.

_____ The flower, which is often brightly colored and scented, grows out of the stem and contains the seeds of the plant.

_____ The leaves, which are attached to the stem, manufacture most of the food for the plant.

_____ Each of the parts plays a role in maintaining the life of the plant.

Building a Paragraph

EXERCISE 4-7.   THE ELEPHANT.   A. The following chart lists the main parts of the African elephant, along with a description of their functions. Study the chart carefully and decide what the name of the function might be. Write the function in the third column. Choose the function from this list.

defense	support
regulation of body temperature	food gathering
communication	

Part	Description of Function	Function
tusks	used to scrape bark from trees used to dig out small trees used to dig for salt used to attack an enemy	
trunk	used to bring food to the mouth used to touch, stroke, and make sounds used to locate enemies and food	
legs	used to trample an enemy used to support the body	
ears	used to cool the body used to frighten the enemy by in- creasing the width of the head	

B. Group the parts according to their common function. That is, list all the parts used in food gathering together, and list all the parts which fit in the other categories in the correct columns.

Food Gathering	Support	Communication	Defense	Regulation of Body Temperature

C. Writing a topic sentence: A paragraph describing the functions of the parts of an elephant would be introduced with a topic sentence that uses some of the key words you learned in the section on the topic sentence. Complete the following sentence and use it as your topic sentence for the paragraph. Choose the word that you think best fits in the sentence.

The different _____ (parts, components) of an elephant have _____ (several, many) functions.

D. Writing the paragraph: Complete the paragraph by adding the correct information describing the function of the parts of the elephant.

The different _____ of an elephant have several _____. The _____ and the _____ are used to gather food. The tusks _____. The trunk is used to _____. The ears, the _____, the tusks, and the _____ are used for defense. The ears are _____. The legs are used to _____, and the tusk is used to _____. The trunk is _____. The body temperature of the elephant is regulated by the _____, which _____. The _____ is used for communication. It _____. Legs are used to _____.

EXERCISE 4-8.   KINDS OF FEATHERS ON A BIRD.   You will be writing a paragraph that classifies the different functions of the feathers of birds. The information is given to you in the chart. Study it carefully, as it contains all the information necessary for you to write sentences for all the steps.

Name of the Feather	Location on the Bird	Function	Appearance
contour feathers	outer part of the body's cover	insulation against weather	soft near the body, stiffer near the tip
down feathers	beneath the contour feathers, close to the skin	insulation against weather	very soft
filoplumes	found mixed with the contour and down feathers	sensory organ for protection	thin and hairlike
flight feathers	wings and tail	helps bird to fly	long, stiff quills

Step 1

Write your topic sentence by completing this statement.

There are four _____ of feathers on a _____.

Step 2

List all the feathers.

_____

_____

_____

_____

Step 3

Classify the feathers by function. Some of the feathers have the same function.

Group 1: Function _____

_____ (name the feather)

_____ (name the feather)

Group 2: Function _____

_____(name the feather)

Group 3: Function _____

_____(name the feather)

Step 4

Describe the function of each group by completing these sentences.

Group 1: The contour feathers and the down feathers *provide insulation against the weather.*

Group 2: Filoplumes help _____ the bird _____.

_____

Group 3: Flight feathers help _____.

_____

Step 5

Describe each example of a feather by telling where it is located and what it looks like.

Contour feathers are located _____

_____.

Down feathers are found _____.

They are _____.

Filoplumes are located _____

_____.

Flight feathers are _____.

They _____.

Step 6

Writing a paragraph: Put your sentences together, beginning with a topic sentence.

Topic sentence: _____.

Describe the functions of Group 1. _____

_____.

Describe the location and appearance of the feathers. _____

_____

_____

_____

Describe the functions of Group 2. _____

_____

Describe the location and the appearance of the feather. _____

_____

_____

Describe the functions of Group 3. _____

_____

Describe the location and the appearance of the feather. _____

_____

EXERCISE 4-9. THE ANT.   A. Study the diagram of the parts of the ant. Fill in the column labeled "Location" with the correct body part.

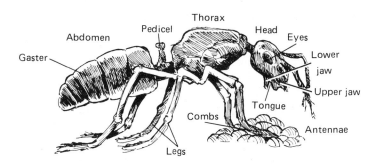

Part	Function	Location
upper jaw	used for grasping, digging, biting	
lower jaw	used for chewing	
antennae	used for feeling and touching	
eyes	used for vision	
tongue	used for licking secretions	
legs	used for locomotion	
combs	used for cleaning	
pedicel	gives the ant mobility	
gaster	contains the crop, digestive organs, sexual glands, and poison glands	

B. Group the parts of the ant according to their location. That is, list all the parts found in the head in one column, the parts found in the thorax in the second column, and the parts found in the abdomen in the third column.

Head	Thorax	Abdomen

C. Writing a topic sentence: Write a topic sentence that tells the number of main parts of the ant. Begin with

There are _____

D. Writing a paragraph: Write your topic sentence at the beginning of the paragraph. Complete the paragraph by describing the different parts of the ant. Describe each section in turn and tell the function of each part.

(Topic sentence) _____

_____

(First part) _____

_____

_____

(Second part) _____

_____

_____

(Third part) _____

_____

_____

_____

EXERCISE 4-10.   CHECKING UP.   A. Choose the correct answer and circle it.

1. When we describe something by *function,* we are describing its (a) appearance, (b) use, (c) location.

2. When we *label* a group of things, we find a word which tells (a) where the things are located, (b) what they have in common, (c) how they are spelled.

3. When we *limit* a topic sentence, we (a) add words to make the sentence longer, (b) add words which will make the topic more specific, (c) take away words to make the sentence shorter.

4. The *order* in which we mention things in a paragraph is often controlled by (a) what has been said in the topic sentence, (b) how we feel at the moment, (c) neither of these things.

B. Write sentences for the following words.

1. permit: _____

2. support: _____

3. manufacture: _____

4. protect: _____

Check your sentences to make sure that your verb agrees with your subject in number.

Five

EXPLAINING PROCESS

This chapter will give you practice in writing paragraphs which describe how to do something. Paragraphs which tell you how to do something are called *process* paragraphs. In order to explain a process, you must put your facts in sequential order of time, called *chronology.* Chronological listing of details means that you put down the things which happened first, second, third, and so on.

If you were changing a tire, for instance, you would have to do several things before you could actually remove and replace the tire, and you would have to do several more things before the job was done. If you were writing a description of the process, you would want to make sure that your reader understood the order in which the job was to be done.

The pre-exercises in the chapter will require you to organize facts logically in terms of time and to recognize steps which are out of order.

The key words and phrases are those which are commonly used to link details together in a process description.

PRE-EXERCISE 5-A.   ORGANIZING FACTS SEQUENTIALLY

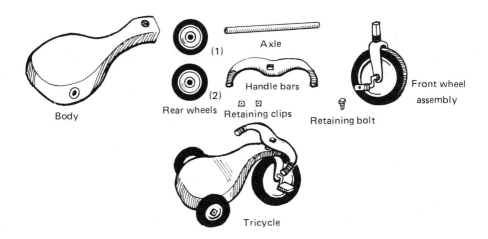

Instructions

Step 1   a.   Place rear wheel 1 on axle.
         b.   Secure with retaining clip.
Step 2   Push rear axle through the holes in the rear of the body.
Step 3   a.   Place rear wheel 2 on axle.
         b.   Secure with retaining clip.
Step 4   Push the front wheel assembly up through the large hole in the front of the body.
Step 5   Place the handlebars over the neck of the front wheel assembly.
Step 6   Secure the handlebars to the front wheel assembly with retaining bolt.

Read the instructions above and answer the questions which follow.

1. What would happen if you did not complete step 1b and step 3b?

    _____

    _____

2. What would happen if you skipped step 2?

    _____

    _____

3. What would happen if you did not complete step 4 before doing step 5?

    _____

    _____

    _____

Note: As you can see from answering these questions, it is very important to follow steps in a process *sequentially*. *Sequentially* means in the correct order from first thing done to last thing done. If you skip one step or do it incorrectly, your explanation will be incomplete.

If you are describing a process, you must be careful to place your details in the correct order. You must also be careful not to leave out any details.

PRE-EXERCISE 5-B. FILLING IN A CHART CHRONOLOGICALLY

History of Transportation

Time	Development	Location
1939	Helicopter first developed by Sikorsky	United States
1930	Jet propulsion principle discovered by _____	_____
_____	First example of powered, controlled flight by an aircraft demonstrated by the Wright brothers	United States
_____	First rigid airship produced by Zeppelin	Germany
1892	First automobile with a carburetor invented by Duryea	United States
_____	First true automobile invented by Panhard and Lavassor	France
1885	_____	Germany
1884	First bicycle built according to principles of today's models	_____
_____	_____	_____
_____	_____	_____

Read the following sentences and complete the chart.

The first bicycle was invented by von Sauerbronn in Germany in 1816. Sixty-eight years later the first bicycle built on modern lines was produced by James Starley in England.

In 1885 the first automobile with an internal combustion engine appeared in Germany. It was built by Benz and Daimler. Six years later in

France, Panhard and Lavassor invented the first true automobile, and the following year Duryea, in the United States, built the first automobile with a carburetor.

The first nonrigid airship was built by Giffard in France in 1852. Forty-eight years later Zeppelin invented the first rigid airship in Germany.

Powered controlled flight began in 1903 as the Wright brothers built in the U S the first fixed-wing aircraft.

By 1930 the principle of jet propulsion had been discovered by Frank Whittle in England.

Nine years later the first helicopter appeared in the United States. It was invented by Sikorsky.

PRE-EXERCISE 5-C.   FINDING AND ORDERING INFORMATION.

The Age of the Dinosaurs

Read the following passage and fill in the chart. You will be looking for specific information and putting it in the correct order.

The Jurassic Period

The Jurassic period began approximately 200 million years ago. During this time the huge plant-eating dinosaurs such as brontosaurus and diplodocus appeared on the earth. These were enormous reptiles that probably spent much of their time eating in order to feed their gigantic bodies. Both dinosaurs had long necks and tails. Brontosaurus was about eighty feet long, and diplodocus was about ninety feet long. These slow-moving beasts had great difficulty protecting themselves from the meat-eating dinosaurs.

Allosaurus was one of the fiercest meat eaters. He was about thirty feet long but stood on his hind legs and was able to move a good deal faster than the two plant eaters. His sharp teeth and claws were well adapted to ripping and tearing flesh.

Some dinosaurs were well protected from enemies like allosaurus. One of these was stegosourus. This plant eater had a double row of bony plates along its back and two spikes near the end of its tail. The spikes could be swung against the legs of an enemy.

The Cretaceous Period

The next period was called the Cretaceous. It began about 135 million years ago. Here we see the development of the ferocious tyrannosaurus rex, a reptile approximately fifty feet long, weighing about ten tons. Its teeth were six inches long and had sharp serrated edges for sawing and pulling flesh.

One of the few dinosaurs that resisted tyrannosaurus rex was tricerotops, a plant eater that had several defenses. One of these was an extension of bone behind the head. Another form of defense was the three sharp horns that grew out of the animal's head and face.

1. Read the passage and underline the dinosaurs in the Jurassic period. Circle the dinosaurs in the Cretaceous period.

2. Write the name of the period in the correct column.

3. Write the names of the dinosaurs in the correct periods.

4. Write plant eater or meat eater in the correct column.

Name of the Period	Name of the Dinosaur	Plant/Meat Eater
(200 million years ago)		
(135 million years ago)		

KEY WORDS AND PHRASES—CHRONOLOGICAL

Starting with Sentences

The following words are used to indicate the steps in a process so that the reader clearly understands what happened first, second, and so on. Study the words and their definitions and do the exercises which follow.

Words commonly used to indicate the first (initial) occurrence:

First of all: First of all, you must read the directions before starting to bake a packaged cake.

First: First you must read the directions before baking a packaged cake.

In the beginning: In the beginning, you must read the directions before baking a packaged cake.

Second: Second you must get out the ingredients.

After that: After that, you must get out the ingredients.

Next: Next you must get out the ingredients.

Then: Then you must get out the ingredients.

Third: Third you should take out a mixing bowl.

After that: After that, you should take out a mixing bowl.

Next: Next you should take out a mixing bowl.

Then: Then you should take out a mixing bowl.

Finally: Finally, you mix the ingredients and put the cake in the oven.

Last: Last you mix the ingredients and put the cake in the oven.

NOTE: *First, second, third,* and *finally* or *last* refer to specific steps in a process. *After that, next,* and *then* are not specific. They cannot be used as connectors, however, unless some step has come before. Try to vary your use of the connectors so that you do not begin each sentence with *then* or *next.*

EXERCISE 5-1. LIGHTING A FIRE

MATERIALS	VERBS
paper	warms
twigs	carries
logs	lights
matches	adds
	puts

A. Write a sentence describing what is going on in each of the pictures. Use the verbs in the list in the correct blanks.

1. (_____) The man _____ the newspaper on the ground.

2. (_____) He _____ the twigs.

3. (_____) He _____ to the fire.

4. (_____) _____

5. (Finally,) _____

B. Which of the following key words and phrases might you use to connect the preceding sentences? Write them in the parentheses before each sentence. You might be able to use more than one key word or phrase.

first	next
second	then
third	finally
first of all	in the beginning
after that	at the end

WRITING A TOPIC SENTENCE

Starting with Sentences

Several words are frequently used in topic sentences for paragraphs which describe how to do something. Study the following words and their definitions.

1. *instructions:* to direct or command; to give knowledge

    I received *instructions* from my doctor on exercising for my health.
    My teacher gives *instructions* before he gives a test.

2. *directions:* to guide or show someone the way

    If I follow the map correctly, I won't need any other *directions.*
    Follow the *directions* on the back of the cake box.

MATERIALS:  = PAPER 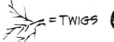 = TWIGS = LOGS 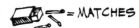 = MATCHES

3. *steps:* to follow a specific course to reach a goal

   You must follow several *steps* in baking a cake.
   To do that math problem, you'll have to do several *steps*.

4. *procedures:* to do specific things to reach a goal (can be used in place of steps)

   Enrolling in school requires that you follow certain *procedures*.
   Every morning I follow the same *procedure* when I get up.

5. *Things:* a very general word which implies that you are to follow certain steps or procedures

   You must do several *things* in baking a cake.
   Every morning I do several *things* when I get up.

EXERCISE 5-2. WRITING A TOPIC SENTENCE.   Study the topics and decide how you would use them in a topic sentence. Remember to use the key words and phrases.

1. changing a diaper _____

_____

2. making a dress from a pattern _____

_____

3. brushing your teeth _____

_____

4. changing the oil in the car _____

_____

ORDERING INFORMATION

Starting with Sentences

You already know that the information in a process paragraph should be ordered chronologically. This means that it should be ordered in a sequence which tells at what time it occurs. The key words and phrases help you to know what order.

EXERCISE 5-3.   USING THE CORRECT ORDER.   Practice using the correct order by rearranging the following sentences. The topic sentence is first. Write the numbers of the sentences at the left in the order in which they fall.

_____   1.   I had a lot of work to do last weekend.

_____   2.   I also weeded the twenty-foot vegetable patch and watered the container plants.

_____   3.   The remaining walls were finished quickly, and I decided to forget about the windows.

_____   4.   I polished and polished until I could see my face in the fenders, and my arm nearly fell off.

_____   5.   Then the rest of the garden had to be attended to.

_____   6.   By then I was exhausted.

_____   7.   First, all the leaves had to be raked and piled up at the curb.

_____   8.   But I concentrated on the ones without windows first and finished them in about forty minutes.

_____   9.   I had to stop and gather my strength before I tackled the windows and walls.

_____   10.   But it was worth it as the car looked marvelous.

_____   11.   The snails had been eating my plants again, so I put out some snail bait.

_____   12.   The walls were more difficult as the area to be covered was great.

_____   13.   After that I had to check the car.

_____   14.   I wasn't happy with the last wash'n'wax job, so I redid it myself.

_____   15.   I was tired.

GIVING AND FOLLOWING DIRECTIONS

Starting with Sentences

EXERCISE 5-4.   USING DIRECTIONS.   To be done as a paired activity in class.

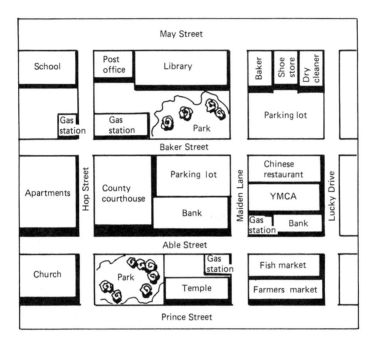

1. Student A calls out the directions for the route from the church to the dry cleaner. Student B traces the route on the map. Student B then gives the map to Student A to check the route.

2. Student B calls out the directions for the route from the farmers market to the post office. Student A traces the correct route and gives the paper to Student B to check for errors.

Building a Paragraph

EXERCISE 5-5.   TAKING A TRIP.   A. You are going to visit friends in another state. You will be gone for a month. There are several last minute things you must do before leaving. Decide in what order you will do these things. Number the steps; then write a sentence for each. Use the first person *I* and the future tense (*will*).

_____ lock the apartment

_____

_____ put suitcase in the car

_____

_____ put gas in the car

_____

_____ take the dog to the neighbor's where it will stay until you return

_____

_____ buy dog food

_____

_____ empty the refrigerator

_____

_____ check the windows

_____

B. Write a topic sentence for a paragraph which would contain the preceding details.

There are several _____

_____

C. Put your topic sentence and the sentences you wrote in A into paragraph form. Add any key words (*first, second, then, after that, finally*) which will make your meaning clearer.

_____

_____

_____

_____

_____

_____

_____

_____

_____

_____

_____

_____

GUIDED IMAGERY.

_____

_____

_____

_____

_____

_____

_____

_____

_____

_____

_____

_____

_____

_____

_____

_____

_____

_____

_____

_____

_____

_____

_____

_____

_____

_____

_____

EXERCISE 5-6. INDEPENDENT ACTIVITY. A. Make notes for a paragraph explaining something you know how to do.

Subject: _____

Steps	Description

B. Write a topic sentence in which you mention the topic and the fact that you will be giving your reader steps to be followed.

There are _____ in _____

_____

C. Write a paragraph made up of complete sentences describing the steps you just outlined. Use the first person (*I*). Make sure that the paragraph is indented. Use the lines which follow.

_____

_____

_____

_____

_____

_____

_____

_____

_____

_____

_____

_____

_____

_____

D. Now mix up the preceding sentences so that they are not in the correct order. When you have finished, fold the paper and exchange it with a friend. See if that person can rearrange the sentences so that they are in the correct order.

_____

_____

_____

_____

_____

_____

_____

_____

_____

_____

_____

_____

_____

EXERCISE 5-7. CHECKING UP.   A. Look at the following topic sentences. Decide what kind of information would appear in the paragraph: descriptive details, details describing function, or details describing process. Write *descriptive, function,* or *process* after each sentence.

1. The large football field was lonely and deserted. _____

2. In the human body most of the parts serve important functions. _____

3. Before taking your driver's test, you must make certain that you can do several things. _____

4. The lake was the loveliest spot I had ever seen. _____

5. Information fed into a computer is processed in several different ways. _____

6. A computer system is made up of several components. _____

7. As I walked down the road, I met a most unusual looking person. _____

8. There are several important tools an artist uses to create a painting. _____

B. Explain the following words.

1. procedure _____

2. process _____

3. step _____

Six

COMPARING
AND CONSTRASTING

In this chapter you will be comparing and/or constrasting things or ideas. *Comparing and contrasting are similar in that you are dealing with things which have some relationship to each other.* In comparing, we emphasize the qualities which are the same. In contrasting, we emphasize the qualities which are different.

You will be doing some pre-exercises which require you to identify similarities or differences. You will also be writing sentences which might be used as topic sentences for comparison-and-contrast paragraphs. You will learn some words which will help your reader understand the direction in which your writing is going.

PRE-EXERCISE 6-A. CLASSIFYING. Look carefully at the following words and cross out the ones which are not similar to the other words.

Example: chair
table
~~orange~~
couch
bed

1. trout
   tuna
   swordfish
   shark
   pig

2. violin
   cello
   piano
   cat
   trumpet

3. rose
   lettuce
   mushroom
   onion
   garlic

4. giraffe
   elephant
   lion
   ostrich
   zebra

5. my
   your
   his
   her
   me

6. cotton
   wool
   steel
   silk
   linen

7. letter
   package
   telegram
   postcard
   Christmas card

8. touch
   taste
   sight
   smell
   running

9. briefcase
   purse
   basket
   handbag
   trunk

10. boots
    shoes
    slippers
    tennis shoes
    gloves

PRE-EXERCISE 6-B.   CLASSIFYING.   Cross out the words in the following lists which are not similar to the other words listed.

1. hotdogs
   hamburgers
   McDonalds
   pizza
   steak

2. pants
   blouse
   skirt
   shirt
   hat

3. cars
   trucks
   bicycles
   vans
   motorcycles

4. highway
   roadway
   train tracks
   river
   footpath

5. robin
   hawk
   goldfish
   airplane
   helicopter

6. sweet
   sour
   bitter
   red
   salty

7. terrible
   awful
   horrible
   wonderful
   ugly

8. large
   small
   tall
   little
   black

9. never
   always
   sometimes
   tomorrow
   there

10. trees
    flowers
    shrubs
    grass
    seaweed

One important thing to remember is that you cannot compare or contrast things which are not alike in any way. Things must have something *in common* in order to be compared. For instance, you would not want to compare a *horse* to a *carrot*. Although they are both living structures, they do not share any other qualities.

PRE-EXERCISE 6-C.   DETERMINING COMPARABLE ITEMS.   From the list choose the things you might be able to compare. Put them on the chart. Then check off the ways in which they might be compared.

chair   window
man   house
dog   vegetable
lamp   wall
couch   rock

Comparable Items	Size	Shape	Function	Color	Category (animal, human, machine, and so on)

KEY WORDS AND PHRASES

Starting with Sentences

EXERCISE 6-1. USING KEY WORDS. Read the following words and their definitions very carefully. A sentence has been written as an example of how to use each word. Write a sentence of your own on the blanks provided beneath each example.

1. relationship: connection between two things or people
   There is a strong relationship between the woman and her daughter.

   _____

   _____

2. resemble: to be like or similar in appearance
   Lettuce and cabbage resemble each other in size, shape, and color.

   _____

   _____

3. approximately the same: nearly the same
   The twins were approximately the same size.

   _____

   _____

4. define: to describe
   Define the meanings of the following words.

   _____

   _____

5. clarify: to make something easier to understand
   He clarified his instructions to the class by drawing a picture on the board.

   _____

   _____

6. generalize: to emphasize the general character of something
   We can generalize about lettuce, cabbage, and spinach by saying that they are all green, leafy vegetables.

   _____

   _____

7. share: to have something in common or alike
   Identical twins share the same physical characteristics.

   _____

   _____

8. compare: to show how things are similar
   The small boy compared his toy car to his father's real car and decided that they were similar.

   _____

   _____

9. contrast: to show how things are different
   The little boy contrasted himself to his brother, who was eighteen years old.

   _____

   _____

SIMILARITIES AND DIFFERENCES

Starting with Sentences

EXERCISE 6-2. NOTING SIMILARITIES.   In describing two items which are alike, you must do two things:

1. Name the similarity.
2. Clarify by describing.

Using the information in the charts, fill in the blanks in the sentences.

Items	Similarity	Clarification
whale	mammal	The mothers supply milk for their young.
porpoise	mammal	The babies develop inside the mothers.

1. Both the _____ and the _____ are _____. The mothers _____, and the babies _____.

Items	Similarity	Clarification
Hawaiians Tahitians	Polynesian Polynesian	They both live in the Pacific.

2. The _____ and the _____ are _____. They both live _____.

Items	Similarity	Clarification
Coca-Cola coffee	brown liquid	They both contain caffeine.

3. Both _____ and _____ are _____. They both _____.

EXERCISE 6-3.   NOTING DIFFERENCES.   The items on the charts are alike in one way and different in another. Fill in the blanks by giving information about how they are alike and then telling how they are different. The words *however* and *but* tell you that you are going to contrast things.

Items	Similarity	Difference
tyrannosaurus rex	dinosaur	meat eater
tricerotops	dinosaur	plant eater

1.   The _____ and the _____ are both _____. However, one is a _____ and one is a _____.

Items	Similarity	Difference
Indian elephant	pachyderm	one "finger" at the end of its trunk
African elephant	pachyderm	two "fingers" at the end of its trunk

2.   The _____ and the _____ are both _____, but the _____ has _____ and the _____ _____ has two.

Items	Similarity	Difference
bee	queen as egg-layer	slender abdomen
ant	queen as egg-layer	fat, swollen abdomen

3.   Both _____ and _____ lay eggs, but their bodies are shaped _____. The _____ has a _____ and the _____ has a _____.

EXERCISE 6-4.   GROUPING LIKE QUALITIES IN A SENTENCE.   A. Look at the following pictures. Then list the similarities you see in the faces.

Similarities

1.   smiles _____

2.   _____

3.   _____

4.   _____

5.   _____

     _____

B.   Write sentences explaining the similarities in the faces. Use the word *all* in each sentence.

Example: *All* the people are smiling.

1.   _____

2.   _____

3.   _____

4.   _____

5.   _____

WRITING TOPIC SENTENCES

Starting with Sentences

When you introduce a paragraph which compares or contrasts, the topic sentence should do two things:

1.   Mention the items being compared or contrasted.
2.   Mention that the paragraph will explain the differences or the similarities.

Usually a paragraph will either compare or contrast.

Some useful words to be used in a topic sentence introducing a paragraph emphasizing similarities are the following:

are alike in
are similar in
can be compared to (with)
there are . . . similarities between

Examples: Plants and animals *are alike in* several ways.
Plants and animals *are similar in* many ways.
Plants *can be compared to* animals in some ways.
There are many *similarities between* plants and animals.

EXERCISE 6-5.   WRITING TOPIC SENTENCES.   A. Look at the following list of suggestions. Think of two specific things which can be compared. Then write four topic sentences, following the preceding patterns, in which you introduce the topics.

Suggestions: two animals
two teachers
two parents

1. _____

2. _____

3. _____

4. _____

If you wanted to emphasize the differences between two items, you might want to use the following words and phrases:

> *are different in*
> *are not alike in*
> *can be contrasted with*
> *there are . . . differences between . . . and . . .*

Examples: Men and women *are different in* several ways.
Men and women *are not alike in* many ways.
Men *can be contrasted with* women in several ways.
There are several *differences between* men and women.

B. Look at the list of suggestions. Think of two specific things which can be contrasted. Then write four topic sentences, following the preceding patterns, in which you introduce the topics.

Suggestions: two children
two cars
two insects

1. _____

2. _____

3. _____

4. _____

EXERCISE 6-6.   IDENTIFYING TOPIC SENTENCES.   Some of the statements below are generalizations which might be used as topic sentences for a comparison/contrast paragraph. They need support to prove them. Some of the sentences are facts. They would not make good topic sentences. Put *TS* in front of the sentences which would make good topic sentences. Put *F* in front of the sentences which would not make good topic sentences. *Be careful.* Some of the sentences are worded differently from the ones on the previous pages (pages 112–113). They contain words which help you to know they are comparison/contrast sentences. Underline the words.

_____   1.   All birds share some characteristics.

_____   2.   A dog has a life span of about twelve years.

_____   3.   Dogs are carnivorous animals.

_____   4.   There are many similarities between squirrels and marmots.

_____   5.   The population of China is over 600,000,000.

_____   6.   Lake Erie is located on the northwestern border of New York State.

_____   7.   All plants have similar structures.

_____   8.   Linen fiber is taken from the stem of the flax plant.

_____   9.   Both cotton and linen share common qualities.

_____ 10.   There are many differences among cats, but they share several specific qualities.

_____ 11.   Japan is located in the northern Pacific Ocean.

_____ 12.   Tokyo is located on the east coast of Japan.

_____ 13.   The Japanese language differs greatly from the English language.

_____ 14.   Although most plants need air, water, and sunlight, some plants do not need as much as others.

_____ 15.   All human beings share certain needs and desires.

_____ 16.   Children need love.

_____ 17.   Eskimos have learned to live comfortably in cold climates.

_____ 18.   Diesel engines are different from gasoline engines in several ways.

_____ 19.   Pigs are intelligent animals.

_____ 20.   There are many differences between private and public education in America.

ORDERING INFORMATION

Starting with Sentences

EXERCISE 6-7.   PUTTING INFORMATION IN ORDER.   A. Key words and phrases help us to put our facts in the logical order. Following are some sentences which, if put together correctly, will make an organized, logical paragraph. Begin by numbering the sentence which would make the best *topic sentence*. Then number the other sentences *in the order in which you think they should come in the paragraph.*

_____ In both areas weather conditions are similar in the summer and fall.

_____ There are similarities and differences in the climate of the south-western part of the United States and that of the southeastern part of the country.

_____ Normally both areas have hot, dry weather in these seasons.

_____ In winter and spring the weather in the Southeast is quite different from the weather in the Southwest, however.

_____ In contrast, winter in the southwestern region is cold and dry, and spring is warm and dry.

_____ Both winter and spring in the southeastern areas are warm and moist.

_____ The two areas are alike in some ways and different in others.

B. Go back and underline all the words which are key words or phrases and helped you understand the order in which the sentences should have been placed.

GUIDED IMAGERY

_____

_____

_____

_____

_____

_____

_____

_____

_____

_____

_____

_____

_____

_____

_____

_____

_____

_____

_____

_____

_____

_____

_____

_____

_____

_____

_____

_____

_____

Building a Paragraph

When you write a comparison-and-contrast paragraph, you need to make sure that your reader knows three things:

1. Whether you are comparing or contrasting (say this in the topic sentence).
2. In what ways (color, size, shape, function, taste, and so on) the items are alike.
3. Specifically what each item looks like, tastes like, is shaped like, or how it functions. You must, in other words, *describe* each item to *clarify* the meaning. The noun for *clarify* is *clarification*.

EXERCISE 6-8.   COMPARING AND CONTRASTING FRUITS.   A. You are all familiar with oranges and grapefruits. They are both *citrus fruits.* Fill in the chart by checking off the ways in which they are (1) similar and (2) different.

1. Similarities

	Size	Shape	Skin Texture	Inner Texture	Color	Taste
Oranges						
Grapefruit						

2. Differences

	Size	Shape	Skin Texture	Inner Texture	Color	Taste
Oranges						
Grapefruit						

B. You want to write a paragraph *comparing* oranges and grapefruit. List the ways in which they are alike.

_____

Write a topic sentence introducing a paragraph comparing the two items.

_____

_____

C. Write the following sentences.

1. Write a sentence that tells the reader the first way in which they are alike. Use the word *shape* in the sentence. _____

_____

2. Write a sentence describing the shape of the orange and grapefruit. <u>Both the orange and grapefruit</u>_____.

3. Write a sentence telling the second way in which they are alike. Use the words *skin texture.*

The _____ and the _____

_____.

4. Write a sentence describing the skin texture of both fruits. _____

_____

5. Write a sentence telling the third way in which they are alike. Use the
    words *inner texture* and *also.*

_____

_____

6. Describe the *inner texture* of the fruits.

_____

_____

D. Put all the sentences which you have written into paragraph form. Do not forget to
indent. Don't forget the topic sentence.

_____

_____

_____

_____

_____

_____

_____

_____

_____

_____

_____

_____

_____

_____

_____

E. Look back at the chart on which you checked off differences. Use the information to write the following sentences.

1. Write a topic sentence which mentions the two fruits and *emphasizes their differences.*

    _____

    _____

2. Write a sentence which tells what the first difference is. Use the word *size.*

    _____

3. Describe the two fruits in terms of their size. Use the word *but.*

    _____ , but _____

    _____.

4. Write a sentence which tells the next difference. Use the word *color* and

    the word *also.* _____

    _____

5. Describe the color of each fruit. Write two sentences.

    _____

    _____

6. Write a sentence which tells what the next difference is. Use the word

    taste. _____

    _____

7. Write a sentence which describes the taste of a grapefruit and the taste of

    an orange. Use the word *but.* The grapefruit _____,

    but the orange _____.

F. Put all the sentences from E together to form a paragraph. Do not forget to *indent.*

    _____

    _____

    _____

    _____

    _____

    _____

_____

_____

_____

_____

_____

_____

_____

EXERCISE 6-9.   CONTRASTING THE BEE AND THE ANT.   A. Look at the information on the chart. It tells the differences between the ant and the bee communities.

	Bee	Ant
Kinds of Food	nectar and pollen	other insects
Leadership	one queen	several queens
Ways of Expanding Their Colonies	queen flies off to a new location and takes half the hive with her	young males and sexual females fly off and mate to create new queens

Bee

Ant

B. Count the number of ways in which the communities are different. Write a topic sentence for a paragraph which would contrast the two communities.

Topic sentence: There are _____ differences between _____.

C. Write your topic sentence on the first line. Then fill in the blank spaces with information from the chart to form a paragraph which contrasts the two communities.

Topic sentence: _____

_____.

They have different kinds of _____. The bee community has

_____ as a leader, but the ant community has _____. They also

eat different kinds of _____. The bees eat _____ but the

_____ eat _____. Finally, they expand their colonies in different ways. The bees _____. The _____. These are the ways in which the communities differ.

(Note: The final sentence is a concluding sentence.)

EMPHASIZING SIMILARITIES AND DIFFERENCES

EXERCISE 6-10.   TWO ISLANDS.   A. The two *islands* in the maps seem to be similar. Study the maps carefully and look at the key and the key words listed under the maps. Then do the exercises.

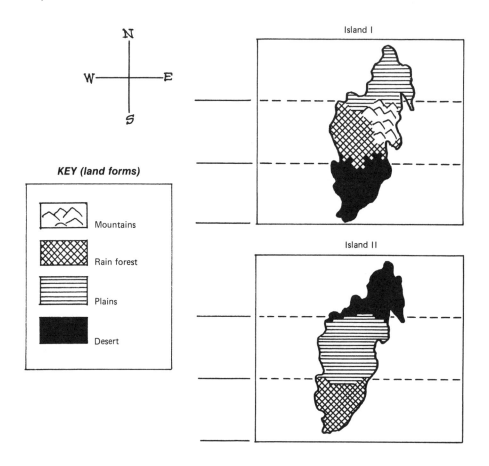

KEY WORDS

northern section	plains	land forms
southern section	mountains	shape
central section	desert	location
island	rain forest	located in

Write a definition for the following key words:

1. island _____

2. plains _____

3. mountains _____

4. desert _____

5. rain forest _____

B. Fill in the blanks with information about the maps.

Similarities

1. They are both maps of _____.

2. The islands are approximately the same _____. They are both (describe shape) _____.

3. They also have many of the same _____ forms. They both have

   _____, _____, and _____.

Differences

1. The main difference between the islands is the location of the _____.

2. Island I has _____ located in the _____ section, but Island II

   has _____

   _____.

3. Island I has _____ located in the _____,

   but Island II has _____

   _____.

4. Another difference is that Island I has _____ located in

   _____. Island II has _____.

5. Island I has mountains located _____, but Island II

   has _____.

C. Write a topic sentence for a paragraph which would emphasize the similarities of the two islands (compare). Use an adjective which indicates how many ways they are alike.

_____

D. Put your topic sentence on the first line. Then use the sentences which you completed under "Similarities" as the body of your paragraph.

_____

_____

_____

_____

_____

_____

_____

_____

_____

_____

_____

E. Write a concluding sentence for the preceding paragraph.

_____

_____

F. Write a topic sentence for a paragraph which would emphasize the differences (contrast) between the two islands.

_____

_____

G. Now take the information listed under "Differences" on page 125 and use it for the body of your paragraph. Put your topic sentence first. _Indent._

_____

_____

_____

_____

_____

_____

_____

_____

_____

H. Write a concluding sentence for the preceding paragraph.

_____

_____

EXERCISE 6-11.   MORE OF TWO ISLANDS

If we want to mention the similarities between two things but *emphasize the differences,* we often use a topic sentence which begins with *although.*

Although the orange and the grapefruit are alike in some ways, they are different in others.

If we want to mention the differences but *emphasize the similarities,* we do the same thing.

Although the orange and the grapefruit are different in some ways, they are alike in others.

A. Write a topic sentence about the two islands in which you mention that they are similar but emphasize the fact that they are different. Begin with the word *although* and follow the pattern in the first example.

_____

B. Write the body of a paragraph which might be introduced by the preceding sentence. First state the ways in which the two islands are alike and then tell how they are different.

_____

_____

_____

_____

_____

_____

_____

_____

_____

_____

_____

_____

_____

C. A good concluding sentence for a paragraph which both compares and contrasts should mention similarities and differences. Choose the sentence which you think would be the best concluding sentence for your paragraph.

1. The greatest similarities between the two islands are found in their shape and in the kinds of land forms they have; the greatest differences are found in the location of the land forms.

2. Therefore Island I is similar to Island II.

3. Island II is different from Island I because it has mountains.

EXERCISE 6-12.   RED SQUIRREL.   A. Read the paragraph and do the exercises which follow.

There are many different kinds of squirrels. They are all rodents. Some members of the squirrel family live in trees. One of the common types of tree squirrel is the red squirrel. Red squirrels are found in the northern forests and make their homes in the hollows of trees or in tree branches. They are usually about one foot in length but can sometimes grow as large as two feet. They do not *hibernate* in the winter although they do stay in their nests during periods when the weather is extremely cold. Red squirrels have long bushy tails which allow them to keep their balance. They are reddish in color. They are most active during the daytime and are *noted for* their harsh and constant scolding and chattering. They prefer to live alone and eat nuts and berries which they find in the woods.

Use each of the following words in a sentence of your own.

1. *hibernate:* to sleep for long periods of time during the winter

   Example: Many animals, such as bears, hibernate during the winter; humans do not.

Your sentence: _____

_____

2. *noted for:* known for; recognized by

   Example: The famous author is noted for his books.

Your sentence: _____

_____

B. Use the following chart to make notes about the red squirrel.

Size	Habitat	Habits	Appearance	Food

Now that you have the information about the red squirrel, do the exercises on pages 132–133. Then combine the information to make a comparison paragraph and a contrast paragraph.

EXERCISE 6-13.   THE MARMOT AND THE SQUIRREL.   A. Read the paragraph and
do the exercises which follow.

Some animals which are related to the squirrel do not live in trees. They
live in underground dens or *burrows*. Hoary marmots are examples of these
relatives of the squirrel. Marmots live in *colonies* of six or more in the high
Rocky Mountain region above the forests of North America. The marmot is
very large compared to the squirrel. A full-grown marmot can weigh around
twenty pounds. It is about thirty inches in length. The marmot has a thick,
reddish-brown coat. It makes a shrill whistle, especially if it wants to warn its
friends of danger. Marmots appear only in the daytime. When the weather gets
cold, they hibernate in underground *dens*. They eat grass and clover which
they find in the high meadows.

Use each of the following words in a sentence of your own.

1. *colonies:* groups of people or animals who live together

> **Example:**   Animals that live together in colonies usually get along
> well with each other.

Your sentence: _____

_____

2. *den:* a cave or other kind of sheltered home for an animal

> **Example:**   The lion lived in a den with his family.

Your sentence: _____

_____

3. *burrow:* an underground home for some animals

    Example: Rabbits and other rodents live in burrows.

Your sentence: _____

_____

B. Use the following chart to make notes about the marmot. Then transfer the information about the squirrel from the chart on page 131.

	Size	Habitat	Habits	Appearance	Food
Hoary Marmot					
Red Squirrel					

C. Count the number of ways in which the red squirrel is similar to the marmot. Write a topic sentence for a paragraph in which you compare the red squirrel with the marmot. Use one of the following adjectives in your topic sentence: *many, some, a few, one, two, three.* Look back at the sentences on page 112 if you have difficulty writing the topic sentence.

_____

D. Now write one sentence *telling* the ways (size, habitat, habits, appearance, group, food) in which the two animals are alike and one sentence *clarifying* the ways in which they are alike. (When you clarify, you are describing.)

1. (Likeness) _____

    (Clarification) _____

2. (Likeness) _____

    (Clarification) _____

3. (Likeness) _____

    (Clarification) _____

E. Use your topic sentence and the other sentences which you wrote to form a paragraph. Do not forget to indent.

_____

_____

_____

_____

_____

_____

_____

_____

_____

_____

_____

F. Write a concluding sentence which summarizes the preceding paragraph.

_____

_____

EXERCISE 6-14.   CONTRASTING RED SQUIRREL AND MARMOT.   A. Look back at
the chart on page 133. Count the ways in which the red squirrel is different from the
marmot. Write a topic sentence for a paragraph in which you contrast the red squirrel
and the marmot. Use one of the following adjectives in your topic sentence: *many,
some, a few, one, two, three.* Look back at the sentences on page 113 if you have
difficulty writing the topic sentence.

Topic sentence: _____

_____

B. Now write one sentence telling each of the ways (size, habitat, habits, appearance,
food) in which the two animals are different and one sentence clarifying the ways in
which they are different. (When you clarify, you are describing.)

1.   (Difference) _____

     (Clarification) _____

2.   (Difference) _____

     (Clarification) _____

3.   (Difference) _____

     (Clarification) _____

4.   (Difference) _____

     (Clarification) _____

5.   (Difference) _____

     (Clarification) _____

C. Write a concluding sentence summarizing the ways in which they are different. (You
might tell how many.)

_____

_____

D. Use your topic sentence and the other sentences which you wrote to form a
paragraph. Do not forget to indent.

_____

_____

_____

_____

_____

_____

_____

_____

_____

_____

_____

_____

_____

_____

_____

_____

EXERCISE 6-15.   CHECKING UP.   Circle the letter next to the sentence that contains the correct meaning of the following words.

1. introduce
    a.   She introduced the paragraph with a concluding sentence.
    b.   Lee was introduced to the class by his teacher.
    c.   The table was introduced by the leg.

2. support
    a.   She supported her new friend to her mother.
    b.   The walls weren't strong enough to support the roof.
    c.   The young man had to support that he didn't commit the crime.

3. prove
    a.   Can you prove that this is the best reason?
    b.   There are many reasons why I can't prove my behavior to you.
    c.   Walls are proved by the foundations.

4. explain
    a.   He explained a piece of fruit from the bowl.
    b.   The parents explained at him.
    c.   The student explained her absence to her teacher.

Fill in the blanks with the correct word: *difference(s)* or *similarity(ies)*.

5.   There are many _____ between identical twins.

6.   There are several _____ to be found among boys who are half-brothers but who have different fathers.

7.   There is a strong _____ between raspberries and strawberries.

8.   Oranges and grapefruit seem to be alike, but there are some _____ between them.

Fill in the blanks with the correct word: *parts, steps,* or *things.*

9.   There are several _____ to be completed in assembling a bicycle.

10.   There are several _____ to consider when taking a vacation.

11.   A paragraph has three _____.

Add a noun to each of the following adjectives to make a phrase.

12.   slender _____

13.   battered _____

14. rectangular _____

15. old _____

Write sentences using the following words.

16. to the right of _____

_____

17. next to _____

_____

18. adjacent to _____

_____

19. in front of _____

_____

Write sentences for the following words.

20. relationship _____

21. resembles _____

22. approximately _____

_____

Seven

USING EXAMPLES TO SUPPORT OR EXPLAIN

We have emphasized description in its various forms in this workbook. You have described the ways things look (size, shape, color, texture, material); you have described things as part of a whole in terms of location and function ("roots are located underneath the ground and support the tree and carry water and minerals to the trunk and branches"); you have told steps in a process (changing the tire on a car); and you have compared and contrasted things (bees and ants).

Another way of describing things is to offer examples or incidents which illustrate the main point which you are making. Examples can be very short (you gave short examples in Chapter 3, "Classification") or they can be long. Examples can be used in any kind of paragraph.

You will be practicing writing examples which are related to main topics in this chapter. These examples may be in the form of incidents or facts.

PRE-EXERCISE 7-A.   RECOGNIZING EXAMPLES.   A. Look at the cartoon frames. Think of as many words as you can to describe what the boy is doing in each frame.

_____

_____

B. What is going on in each picture can serve as an example of *behavior brought about by fear.* Using the following topic sentence and the information in the pictures, write several sentences describing the ways in which the emotion can be expressed.

(Topic sentence) _____ can be expressed in several ways. For example, some people _____

_____.

Other people _____.

Another way to express _____ is to _____

_____.

(Concluding sentence) People respond to _____ in different ways.

PRE-EXERCISE 7-B. THINKING OF EXAMPLES.   Think of as many examples as you can to illustrate or explain the following topics.

1. Irritating characteristics of another person

   Example: rudeness

   _____

   _____

   _____

2. Good qualities of another person

   _____

   _____

   _____

   _____

3. Difficulties in registering for school

   _____

   _____

   _____

   _____

4. Advantages of living where you do

   _____

   _____

   _____

5. Difficulties of shopping in a supermarket

   _____

   _____

   _____

   _____

PRE-EXERCISE 7-C. GIVING COMPLETE EXAMPLES. A. Choose one of the qualities which you listed in number 2 on the preceding page. Write a full explanation by giving an example of how this person behaves.

> **Example:** Gloria is very kind. If I am in trouble in any way, she is willing to listen to me and to try to help me solve my problem. (Note: The quality has been named and explained specifically.)

Your example and explanation: _____

_____

_____

_____

_____

_____

_____

B. Choose one of the difficulties which you listed in number 3. Describe an incident which occurred. Tell *where it happened, who was involved, what happened,* and *how it ended.*

_____

_____

_____

_____

_____

_____

_____

_____

_____

_____

_____

_____

KEY WORDS AND PHRASES

Starting with Sentences

The most commonly used words and phrases which tell the reader that an example is going to be used are the following:

> **for example**
> **for instance**
> **an (one) illustration of . . .**

For example and *for instance* often come at the beginning of the sentence:

> *For example,* one year I had a lot of trouble with my car.
> *For instance,* I had a lot of trouble with my car.

An illustration is usually followed by *of:*

> *An illustration of* his poor study habits was his insistence on listening to very loud music while he ate banana ice cream and cookies and did his math.

EXERCISE 7-1. WRITING EXAMPLES.   Look at the following sentences and write an example for each topic.

1. Learning English poses many problems for me. For example, it is difficult to _____

    _____

2. Registration at a new college presents a number of problems for the new students. An illustration of this would be _____

    _____

3. There are several ways to cook eggs. For instance, you can _____

    _____

TOPIC SENTENCES

Starting with Sentences

Words like *always, sometimes, frequently,* and *some* seem to suggest to the reader that one or more examples will be used in the paragraph.

EXERCISE 7-2. EXAMPLE OR DESCRIPTION.   A. Some of the following sentences might be best developed by giving clear descriptive details; others might be best developed by giving one or more examples to illustrate or prove the topic. Study the sentences. Put an *E* in front of the sentences which you think need to have one or more examples to prove them. Put a *D* in front of the sentences which you feel need only descriptive details.

_____	1.	My father has always found ways to show us he loves us.
_____	2.	Sometimes it pays to be honest.
_____	3.	Good friends frequently save us from embarrassing situations.
_____	4.	Tom is a handsome man.
_____	5.	There are six components in a stereo system.
_____	6.	John has always been a difficult child.
_____	7.	John is tall, dark, and handsome.
_____	8.	Children sometimes teach their parents important lessons.
_____	9.	Some people look like their pets.
_____	10.	That man looks like his dog.

B. Choose three of the preceding sentences. Think of one or more incidents or examples which might illustrate the main idea. Write your examples on the blanks. Use complete sentences.

1. _____

_____

_____

2. _____

_____

_____

3. _____

_____

_____

C. Listed are three of the topics which you used in Pre-exercise 7-B. Write a topic sentence for each, using the key word in parentheses following the topic.

1. Difficulties in registering for school (*sometimes*)

    _____

    _____

2. Irritating characteristics of another person (*some*)

    _____

    _____

3. Difficulties of shopping in a supermarket (*frequently*)

    _____

    _____

(Note: If you have difficulty, look back at page 145 to see how these words are used in topic sentences.)

SUPPORTING BY INCIDENT

Building a Paragraph

In doing the following exercises, follow these steps:

Step 1: Think of an incident which will prove or explain the topic.
Step 2: Write the incident out as if you were telling it to a friend. Don't simply list it as an example. Tell it as a story.

Example 1: Here is an incident which proves the following saying: "All that glitters is not gold." The literal meaning of this saying is that something that looks good may not necessarily be all that it appears to be.

Incident as proof: In buying vegetables in the supermarket, I found an avocado which was large, shiny, and bright green. I took it home and was anxious to cut it up and serve it in a salad for dinner. As soon as I pricked it with a knife, however, I was disappointed. Inside, the fruit was grainy and soft. It smelled spoiled. I finally had to throw the whole thing away. Even though it looked delicious on the outside, inside it was no good.

Question: How does this incident prove the idea expressed in the saying? __

_____

_____

Example 2:   "You can lead a horse to water, but you can't make him drink." The literal meaning of this saying is that you can give someone all the opportunities for success, but you can't make the person successful.

Incident as proof: My son is very bright. He has a high intelligence, but he doesn't do well in school. I have paid a lot of money for private teachers to help him; I have sent him to two private schools because I thought that the education was better than it was in the public school. I have bought him books and encyclopedias to help him with his work. I even bought him an expensive computer and some computer tapes. Still he does not do well in school. I have given him all the opportunities, but I cannot make him succeed.

Question: How does this incident prove the idea expressed in the saying? __

_____

_____

EXERCISE 7-3. USING INCIDENTS TO SUPPORT. Following are some sayings and explanations of their meanings. *Think of an incident which you might use to illustrate the truth of the statements.* Then describe the incident.

"Love is blind." Literal meaning: We do not always see things as they really are if we are involved emotionally.

Your incident as proof: _____

_____

_____

_____

_____

_____

_____

_____

_____

"A stitch in time saves nine." Literal meaning: If you take care of a problem when it first occurs, it will probably not grow larger.

Your incident as proof: _____

_____

_____

_____

_____

_____

_____

_____

_____

In the following exercises you will work through a process which will give you more than one example for each topic. You will also practice writing topic sentences which could be used to introduce a paragraph developed by example.

EXERCISE 7-4.   SUPPORTING WITH TWO OR MORE EXAMPLES.   A. People show their grief (sorrow) in different ways. Give examples of the way you might imagine (or know) each of the following people would show grief. What might each *do* to express the emotion?

1.   Yourself: I express grief or sorrow by _____.

2.   Your mother (father, sister, brother, wife, or husband): My _____ expresses grief by _____.

3.   Your best friend: My best friend expresses grief by _____

_____.

B. Since you have made up more than one example, you will want to use the key words *several* or *different* in your topic sentence. Complete the following topic sentence.

People express their grief in _____

_____

C. Put your topic sentence together with your example sentences to form a paragraph. Use the phrase *for example* with the first sentence.

_____

_____

_____

_____

_____

_____

_____

_____

_____

_____

_____

D. Choose the concluding sentence which you think would summarize this paragraph best.

1. I don't like grief.

2. There are many ways of expressing grief or sorrow.

3. These are just three examples of the kinds of reactions people have to grief.

Add the concluding sentence to the preceding paragraph.

EXERCISE 7-5. SUPPORTING WITH TWO OR MORE EXAMPLES. A. People have different dreams of how they would spend their money if they had a lot of it. Give an example of the way you might imagine (or know) each of the following people would spend $1 million. Make your examples general—for example, travel, clothing, new house, education, helping others. Follow the sentence pattern in the first sentence.

1. You: If I had a lot of money, I would spend it on _____.

2. Your best friend: If _____ had a lot of money, _____
    _____.

3. Your wife (husband, mother, father, sister, brother):
    _____
    _____.

B. Now be specific. For instance, if you said that you would spend your money on travel, where would you like to go? Give details to support your examples.

1. (You) _____
    _____
    _____

2. (Your best friend) _____
    _____
    _____

3. (Your wife, husband, and so on) _____
    _____
    _____
    _____

C. Think of a topic sentence which could be used to introduce this paragraph. Use *people* as the subject for the sentence.

_____

D. Think of a concluding sentence which might summarize this paragraph.

_____

E. Write your topic sentence, your body sentences, and your concluding sentence. Do not forget to indent.

_____

_____

_____

_____

_____

_____

_____

_____

_____

_____

_____

_____

GUIDED IMAGERY.

_____

_____

_____

_____

_____

_____

_____

_____

_____

_____

_____

_____

_____

_____

_____

_____

_____

_____

_____

_____

_____

_____

_____

_____

_____

_____

_____

_____

_____

_____

EXERCISE 7-6.   CHECKING UP.   In the following sets of statements, choose the most specific example to support the topic.

1. My brother is often mean to me.
    a. He is twelve years old and doesn't know any better.
    b. He often plays tricks on me.
    c. One time he put grease on the doorknob of my bedroom so that I had a lot of trouble getting out.

2. I prefer American food to the food in my country.
    a. It tastes good.
    b. One example of the kind of American food I like is the hamburger. It can be eaten in a bun or without a bun and has a nice texture and taste.
    c. All American foods are greasy, and I like greasy foods.

3. People have shown me their kindness in many ways.
    a. They seem to like me.
    b. On buses, for instance, men will almost always get up and offer me a seat.
    c. I appreciate what they do for me.

4. Sometimes I have a hard time saying what I want to say.
    a. I wish I didn't have so much trouble.
    b. If I have to speak in front of a large group of people, I suddenly forget everything I know.
    c. I get frightened, I guess.

5. Frequently, I get angry with my son.
    a. He doesn't get his homework done on time.
    b. He is rude to me and doesn't follow my instructions.
    c. Sometimes I get so mad at him that I have to leave the room to cool down.
    d. I get angry with him when he doesn't pick up his clothes, for instance.

Eight

USING REASONS
TO SUPPORT
YOUR OPINION

You are often asked to give your opinion and to support it with *reasons.* To do this effectively, you need to use many of the thinking skills which you have been practicing in this workbook. You need to *observe, to classify and label, to compare and contrast, to describe and give examples, and to see things in relation to each other and as parts of the whole.*

In this chapter you will be doing some pre-exercises on distinguishing between fact and opinion and some exercises which will help you to express opinions and give reasons. You will also learn how to organize your information.

Some of the writing exercises will be arranged so that you are given facts and must give your opinion based on the facts. Others will be arranged so that you give your opinion on a topic and then your reasons for feeling as you do.

PRE-EXERCISE 8-A.   FORMING AN OPINION

1. Look at the illustrations. Which would you choose if you were buying
    them? _____

A.   B.

    Write a sentence which explains your choice. <u>I would choose . . . because</u>

    _____.

2. You need a car for personal transportation, but you can only afford to
    spend $1,000. You have a choice of two purchase plans. Which would you
    choose if you want to spend the least amount of money?

    PLAN 1
      a. $500 payable immediately
      b. $500 financed over one year at 10 percent interest

    PLAN 2
      a. $300 payable immediately
      b. $800 financed over one year at 8 percent interest

    Explain why you chose the plan you did. _____

    _____

    _____

    _____

3. You are in charge of deciding where to construct a bridge connecting two of
    the cities on the map. Look at the map and study the list of facts about the
    cities. Then decide where you would construct the bridge.

    FACTS ABOUT THE CITIES
    City A: 200,000 people
            three large industries
            municipal airport
    City C: 300,000 people
            no industry

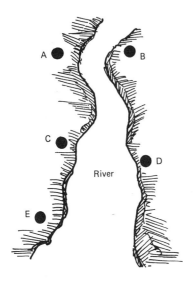

City E: 100,000 people
        no industry
City B: 100,000 people
        railroad passes through city
        no industry
City D: 300,000 people
        four large industries
        railroad passes through city

Explain why you would build a bridge between two of the cities.

I would construct the bridge between city _____ and city

_____ for the following reason(s). _____

_____

_____

_____

_____

_____

_____

_____

_____

_____

_____

_____

PRE-EXERCISE 8-B.   GIVING A REASON.   The following groups of words have something in common. Write a sentence which tells the reason they are alike. Use the word *because* in your explanation.

_____ 1. glasses   _____, _____, d _____ are

           telescope   alike because _____ _____
           binoculars _____.

_____ 2. crayon   A _____, a piece of _____ and a _____
           chalk
           pencil   _____.

_____ 3. snow   _____
           ice
           hail   _____

                       _____.

_____ 4. bark   _____
           skin
           fur   _____

                       _____.

DISTINGUISHING BETWEEN FACT AND OPINION

Starting with Sentences

We use certain words when we are expressing an opinion. These words should help you to distinguish between statements which are *facts* and statements which are *opinions*. The following words are sometimes used to tell your reader that you are expressing an opinion.

> *think: I think* that that girl is beautiful.
> *I think* that the problem could be solved if the two sides would talk about it.
> (Both the statements express opinions rather than truths.)
> *in my opinion: In my opinion,* you are wrong.
> *In my opinion,* this car will be your best choice.

These words are signal words for your reader. They clearly indicate that what will follow will be an opinion. Some sentences contain other words which also mean that they are opinions. Some common verbs that indicate opinion are *love, hate, approve, disapprove, like, dislike.*

> I *hate* (or *love*) your new dress.
> I *disapprove* of the way you eat.
> I *approve* of your appearance.
> I *like* peas.
> I *dislike* cabbage.

Adjectives which express some emotion or feeling are also clues to opinions.

The movie was *fascinating*.
(This is one person's opinion. Someone else might disagree.)
It's *uncomfortable* in this room.
(This is one person's reaction to the room. Someone else might be perfectly comfortable.)

EXERCISE 8-1. FACT OR OPINION.   A. In the following sentences, decide if the adjective makes the statement an opinion or a fact. Circle the adjectives which make the statements opinions.

1. Your dress is *ugly*.

2. The house next door is *blue*.

3. That man is *tall*.

4. The price of that suit is too *high*.

5. That is a *reasonable* request for you to make.

B. Look at the following statements. Some of them are facts and some are opinions. Put *F* after the ones which are facts. Put *O* after the ones which are opinions.

1. Dogs are carnivorous animals. _____

2. I think there should be stricter rules about keeping dogs off the streets. _____

3. I think that the welfare system is the most effective way of making sure that everyone has enough to eat. _____

4. I think the welfare system is unfair. _____

5. The welfare system is unfair. _____

6. The welfare system provides assistance to those who can prove that they need it. _____

7. Our house is 100 years old. _____

8. Our house needs to be redecorated. _____

9. If you love children, you will love this movie. _____

10. The movie is about children. _____

11. The park has an officer who patrols every night. _____

12. Purple is an ugly color. _____

13. Purple is a color which can be made by mixing blue and red. _____

14. People who hate cold weather will hate Maine. _____

15. Several states in the United States have temperatures below zero in the winter. _____

16. You are an uncaring person. _____

17. The temperature today was thirty degrees according to the thermometer.
_____

18. Peas are part of the legume family. _____

19. You'll love my dog. _____

20. All dogs make good pets. _____

TOPIC SENTENCES

Starting with Sentences

EXERCISE 8-2. LIMITING SENTENCES.   A. The following sentences could be topic sentences for a paragraph developed by reasons. Circle the general topic and underline the limiting part of each sentence. The limiting part will be the part of the sentence which suggests that you will be giving *reasons* in the body of the paragraph.

> **Example:** I do not like string beans for several reasons.
>
> *Explanation: String beans* is the topic. *Reasons for not liking them* is the limiting part.

1. I don't think the government should have a policy of taxing the poor.

2. I hate winter sports.

3. I like team sports for several reasons.

4. A cooking class is the best way to learn to cook.

5. It is impossible to grow roses in the winter in the Eastern States.

6. There are several reasons why I chose to go to college.

B. Some of the preceding topic sentences mention the word *reason(s)*. List the numbers of these sentences on the following blank.

_____

THINKING OF REASONS

Starting with Sentences

EXERCISE 8-3.   ADDING REASONS.   Think of reasons that will complete the following sentences.

1. I didn't register for an English class this semester because _____

_____

2. I can't drive my car today because _____

3. Palm trees don't grow in the arctic because _____

4. My parents don't speak English because _____

5. We have to leave early because _____

6. I bought the wrong book because _____

7. My plane arrived two hours late because _____

8. I needed an extra pen because _____

ORDERING INFORMATION

Starting with Sentences

The key words and phrases for a paragraph developed by reason are nearly the same as the key words and phrases for a process paragraph. The most common of these words are the following:

First of all; first: indicating that this is your first reason
Second of all; second: indicating that this is your second reason
Most important of all: pointing out to your reader that this is your most important reason
Finally: emphasizing importance or indicating that this is the final reason

EXERCISE 8-4.   ORDERING REASONS.   Usually you choose the most important reason in your argument and put it last. This means that your reader will remember it best. Look at the following sets of reasons. Decide which you think is the most important reason. Then decide which is the least important reason. Put the words *most important* and *least important* after these reasons.

1.   Reasons for buying a new car

    a.   looks _____

    b.   price _____

    c.   comfort _____

2.   Reasons for attending school

    a.   knowledge _____

    b.   means to gain a job _____

    c.   meet new people _____

3.   Reasons for getting married

    a.   love _____

    b.   financial security _____

    c.   children _____

Study the organizational chart and then do the exercise which follows.

ORGANIZATION-FOR-REASON PARAGRAPH

Topic sentence: gives opinion.	*I like string beans for several reasons.*
Reason 1: supports opinion. Explanation or example: explains reason.	*They are convenient. They can be stored in the refrigerator for quite a while, and they are fast and easy to cook.*
Reason 2: supports opinion. Explanation or example: explains reason.	*They are inexpensive. They cost only about ten cents a serving.*
Reason 3: supports opinion. Explanation or example: explains reason.	*They are nutritious. They contain protein.*
Concluding sentence: summarizes.	*Because of their convenience, cost, and nutritional value, I think string beans are excellent.*

EXERCISE 8-5.   RECOGNIZING KEY WORDS AND PHRASES.   Read the following passage and answer the questions which follow it.

> I hated the room for several reasons. *First of all,* it was hot. There were a lot of people crowded together in the room and their bodies gave off a warm, moist heat which was unpleasant. *Second,* it was ugly. The walls were gray and bare, and the windows were dirty. Some of the window panes were broken. *Most important of all,* the room smelled bad. The air was filled with the odor of perspiration and strong perfume. After being there for ten minutes, I could hardly wait to get out.

1.   The writer stated three reasons and explained them. He used adjectives for
       ~ach reason statement. Write the words on the

       _____   _____

2.   Put parentheses around   which explain the reasons.

3.   Look at the topic sentence.   ~at to expect in the

       paragraph? _____   _____

(Note: Each reason was followed by an explanation.   a reason standing alone in a paragraph. It must be supported by specific   explanation to prove it.)

Building a Paragraph

EXERCISE 8-6. REASONS FOR PREFERRING A WARM CLIMATE. A. The following sentences could be the body of a paragraph which explains reasons for preferring a warm climate. Read the sentences carefully. Three of them are stated as reasons. The rest of the sentences are specific examples to support each of the reasons. Label the sentences.

1. When I live in a warm climate, I enjoy better health. _____

2. Winter clothes are expensive. _____

3. In a warm climate I can enjoy my favorite kinds of recreation all year round. _____

4. I haven't had a cold in over three years. _____

5. A warm jacket costs about half the price of a heavy winter coat. _____ _____

6. In a warm climate, I can reduce my expenses. _____

7. I can swim, play tennis, and ride my bicycle all year round. _____

8. Heating costs less in a warm climate, also. I can heat my house for about one-third the price of heating in a cold climate. _____

9. I can play soccer and basketball outdoors even in winter. _____

B. Write a topic sentence to introduce this paragraph. Look back at the examples on page 162 if you have difficulty.

_____

C. Decide which of the reason sentences you think is least important, next important, and most important. Add the key words *first, second,* and *most important of all* to the sentences and write them on the blanks.

_____

_____

_____

_____

_____

_____

_____

_____

_____

D. A concluding sentence for this paragraph might include a mention of the three *reasons*. Complete the following sentence and use it for your concluding sentence.

I prefer to live in a warm climate because _____

_____

E. Put the topic sentence together with the reason and explanation sentences and the concluding sentence to form a paragraph.

_____

_____

_____

_____

_____

_____

_____

_____

_____

_____

_____

_____

_____

_____

EXERCISE 8-7.   CHOOSING THE BEST JOB APPLICANT

Want Ad

PROGRAMMER TRAINEE. Following qualifications necessary: must be a fast learner; work well with others; be able to take direction. Know one or more computer languages (COBOL and/or BASIC). Be familiar with control language of one or more machines. Some formal background in computer theory desirable. Send resume qualifications to Box 8188. EOE.

A. Read the want ad. Study the summarized résumés of two applicants and decide which person you feel would be most qualified for the job. Explain in complete sentences why you chose the person. Use the chart to help you organize your thoughts.

Applicant 1

Lilia Valencia has a certificate in computer science from a local junior college. She had excellent grades, works fast, but has no experience. She owns her own APPLE computer and has designed programs for her personal use. She is willing to learn, but she has not had supervisory experience. She prefers to work independently.

Applicant 2

Lee Jones has had two years' experience as a computer operator for the city. He has been a shift supervisor with lower-management responsibilities in overseeing machines and shift personnel. He is familiar with planning tapes and implementing daily runs. He has had two night school classes in computer science and is presently taking a class in COBOL. He is reliable, cooperative, and well liked by the people with whom he works.

Fill in the chart.

	Training	Experience	Personality
Valencia			

	Training	Experience	Personality
Jones			

B. After you have decided which of the applicants you think would be best, write a topic sentence for a paragraph in which you will give reasons for your choice.

_____

_____

C. Write sentences giving your reasons and explaining them.

Reason _____

Explanation _____

_____

_____

Reason _____

Explanation _____

_____

_____

Reason _____

_____

Explanation _____

_____

_____

D. Write a concluding sentence for the paragraph.

_____

_____

E. Put all your sentences together to form a paragraph.

_____

_____

_____

_____

_____

_____

_____

_____

_____

_____

_____

EXERCISE 8-8.   OLDER PEOPLE IN NURSING HOMES.   A. Choose one of the sides of the following topic. Then follow the directions for writing a paragraph.

Topic: Older people in nursing homes
Side 1: Older people should be placed in nursing homes.
Side 2: Older people should live with their children.

List the reasons for your opinion. Then write one or two sentences of explanation or give an example to support your reason.

Reason 1 _____

_____

Explanation or example _____

_____

Reason 2 _____

_____

Explanation or example _____

_____

Reason 3 _____

_____

Explanation or example _____

_____

(Note: If you cannot think of three reasons, you may give two.)

B. Decide what order you will use to list the reasons and explanations or examples in your paragraph. Write a sentence for each reason you have listed. Begin your sentence with one of the key words or phrases (*first, second, most of all,* or *finally*).

_____

_____

_____

_____

_____

_____

_____

_____

_____

_____

C. Write a topic sentence for your paragraph. You may use one of the preceding sentences if you wish.

_____

_____

D. Write all your sentences on the following blanks. Do not forget to indent.

_____

_____

_____

_____

_____

_____

_____

_____

_____

_____

_____

E. Add a concluding sentence to the preceding paragraph.

_____

_____

EXERCISE 8-9.   OLDER MEN MARRYING YOUNGER WOMEN.   A. Choose one of the sides of the topic. Then follow the directions for writing a paragraph.

Topic: Older men marrying younger women
Side 1: Older men should marry younger women.
Side 2: Older men should not marry younger women.

List the reasons for your opinion. Then write one or two sentences of explanation or give an example to support your opinion.

Reason 1 _____

_____

Explanation or example _____

_____

Reason 2 _____

_____

Explanation or example _____

_____

Reason 3 _____

_____

Explanation or example _____

_____

(Note: If you cannot think of three reasons, you may give two.)

B. Decide what order you will use to list the reasons and explanations or examples in your paragraph. Write a sentence for each reason you have listed. Begin your sentence with one of the key words or phrases (*first, second, most of all, finally*).

_____

_____

_____

_____

_____

_____

C. Write a topic sentence for your paragraph.

_____

_____

D. Write all your sentences on the following blanks. Do not forget to indent.

_____

_____

_____

_____

_____

_____

_____

_____

_____

_____

_____

_____

_____

E. Add a concluding sentence to the preceding paragraph.

_____

_____

GUIDED IMAGERY.

_____

_____

_____

_____

_____

_____

_____

_____

_____

_____

_____

_____

_____

_____

_____

_____

_____

_____

_____

_____

_____

_____

_____

_____

_____

_____

_____

EXERCISE 8-10.   CHECKING UP

Explain the kinds of information which you must include in a reason paragraph. _____

_____

What does a concluding sentence do in a reason paragraph?

_____

In expressing my opinion, what might I say at the beginning of a sentence?

_____

Why do I need to give an explanation or example after every reason? _____

_____

Instructor's Manual

Thinking/ Writing

An Introduction to the Writing Process for Students of English as a Second Language

by Martha Kilgore Rice and Jane Unaiki Burns

B. Kobus

Instructor's Manual

THINKING/WRITING

An Introduction to the Writing
Process for Students of English
as a Second Language

Martha Kilgore Rice/Jane Unaiki Burns
San Joaquin Delta College

Prentice-Hall, Englewood Cliffs, New Jersey 07632

CONTENTS

PREFACE

The Teacher's Guide for THINKING/WRITING contains suggestions for class activities, scripts for the guided imageries, and answers to some of the more complicated exercises that appear in the book. Our suggestions have come from our own experiences with our students, and we hope that you will find them helpful. As you teach the book, you will undoubtedly come up with additional activities to meet the special needs of your students.

Martha Kilgore Rice
Jane Unaiki Burns

Chapter I - THE PARAGRAPH AS A WHOLE UNIT

<u>Skills</u>: Recognition of the parts of the paragraph and their functions.

Note: The first chapter introduces the concept of the paragraph.
Many students will find this a difficult concept to grasp at first, and it is
not expected that they fully understand the nature of paragraph development at
this point. We feel, however, that it is important to introduce the students
to the principal parts of the paragraph and their functions at the outset.

<u>Starting with sentences</u> (pgs. 3, 5, 6, 8, 10, 11; exercises 1-1, 1-3, 1-4, 1-6
1-9) Understanding the key words and phrases and being able to demonstrate
this understanding in writing is crucial to the students' mastery
of the material. It is worthwhile, therefore, to take the time to discuss each item in depth. Have the students write their first sentences
on the board and use this time to review sentence patterns.
        In exercise 1-3 on page 5, students must identify words which are
important in the topic sentences and in exercise 1-4 on page 6, they should be
using these key words to write their own sentences. Exercises 1-6 on page 8,
1-8 on page 10, and 1-9 on page 11 also give the students practice in
recognizing and using key words in their own sentences.

<u>Building a Paragraph</u> (pgs. 3, 7, 9, 12; exercises 1-2, 1-5, 1-7)
        These exercises deal with recognition of the the kinds of elements
necessary in a well-organized paragraph.

<u>Guided Imagery</u> (pg. 13)
        This exercise gives the students their first practice in independent
writing. You may wish to take the whole class through a series of relaxation
exercises first or simply follow the directions below. In having the students
relax, it is sometimes helpful to play music on a tape recorder. Almost any
soothing music will do, but classical music is often the most effective.
While exercises of this sort are best done with eyes closed, some students may
not wish to close their eyes. It really doesn't matter. What does matter is
that they relax and listen carefully to what you are telling them. Ask them
to close their eyes if they wish, to take a deep breath or two, to uncross
their legs and to sit comfortably. When you feel that they are ready, you may
begin the script. The elipsis marks indicate pauses, and it is important to
pause for enough time to let the students visualize what you are saying.

        Sit comfortably in your chairs....uncross your legs...close your eyes if
you wish....now take a deep breath and hold it while I count to three...one,
two, three...now breathe out and let your whole body relax....forget about
all of the problems which you may have...think only about this moment...take
another deep breath...hold it...now exhale...let your mind relax...imagine
that you are in a market...you are looking for the produce section....you see
the fruits and vegetables...move closer to the counter where the fruits and
vegetables are...pick up a piece of fruit...hold it in your hand...feel its
weight...how does it feel...what kind of a fruit is it....is it large or
small...look at it closely....what color is it....what does it feel like...is
it firm or soft...what does the skin feel like....is it soft...is it rough...
bumpy...smooth....pitted....what shape is the fruit....is it round....is it
long and thin...is it oval in shape...look at the number of parts...is there a
stem....is it stemless...smell the fruit...does it have a smell...is it
sweet....sour....does it smell like anything else that you can think of....now
put the fruit back in the bin and look at it once again...on the count of
three open your eyes...one...two...three...now open your eyes....

Directions: Now write about the piece of fruit which you have imagined.
Begin your paragraph with the following sentence: The piece of fruit which I
imagined was the _____ . Then describe it as fully as you
possibly can. Think of how large it was, how much it weighed, what color it
was, what shape it was, how it smelled.

One way to deal with these early papers is to collect them and read the
descriptions to the class. See if the students can guess from the description
what the fruit was. Discuss the kinds of details that might have been added
to create a clearer picture of the fruits.

Exercise 1-11, pg. 14.
    Answers to Checking Up

    1. Answers will vary. See page 4 in text.

    2. Answers will vary. A topic sentence introduces the paragraph.
    3. Relevant information is necessary information.
    4. The concluding sentence summarizes the paragraph.
    5. three

Part	Function
topic sentence	introduces the paragraph
body	supports the topic sentence
concluding sentence	summarizes the paragraph

Chapter II - WRITING DESCRIPTIVE PARAGRAPHS

Skills: Defining qualities, categorizing, defining spatial relationships, making simple generalizations.

Pre-exercises (pgs. 17, 18; pre-exercises 2-a, 2-b)
    In these exercises, the students name basic qualities, particularly size and shape. If necessary, review the basic shapes--square, circle, triangle, oval, rectangle, etc. You might want to bring in items of different shapes. Discuss adjective and noun forms for the "shape" words, e.g. rectangle, rectangular. Fruits make very good examples, and they are useful when discussing three-dimensional names, e.g. globe, sphere, cube, etc. Other useful tools for eliciting vocabulary discussion are quisinaire rods. They are good for discussing size, shape, color, as well as for comparison and contrast. Students should be encouraged to be as precise as possible in their descriptions. Introduce phrases used in comparisons, e.g. It is shaped like a baseball; It is shaped like a box. Some of the objects in the exercises can be viewed in more than one way. As long as the student can support his/her answer logically, the answer should be considered to be correct.

Starting with Sentences (pgs. 20-27; exercises 2-2, 2-3, 2-4, 2-5)
    We have found that a great many students have difficulty with adjective placement. If your students already have a firm grasp of word order, then omit the early exercises and go on to exercise 2-4 on page 25.
You may want to review what was said about topic sentences in Chapter I before doing this exercise. The important concept for the students to understand here is that topic sentences for descriptive paragraphs contain words that are general and can be enhanced by specific details in the body of the paragraph itself.
    When they begin writing topic sentences, students can refer to the sample sentences on page 24 for word order, or if you wish to extend the exercise, you can offer them variations. In exercise 2-5, the students are to use three of the topic sentences they wrote on page 25. Because they must choose details which fit with the topic sentences they use, this is a good time to review relevant, support, prove, and explain.

Building a Paragraph (pgs. 27-39; exercise 2-6 through 2-14)
    Have the students study the illustration and identify the whole and its parts. Discuss size, shape, location of parts and number of parts. Emphasize the fact that the vocabulary must be as precise as possible. A topic sentence has been started for them and mentions number and shape. They are to fill in the details on the marked lines before they begin to write. This may be done as a group exercise if the class is not very advanced. Before having the students do exercise 2-9 on page 29, discuss vocabulary related to the body, e.g. skin tones may be ruddy, sallow, creamy, tanned, etc. Assist the students in writing the topic sentence, if necessary. Before doing the work on pages 30 and 31, the students should discuss the key words and phrases. In exercise 2-12 on page 34, everything should be described in relationship to the globe, which is the central figure in the drawing. If the students begin by stating that the globe is located in the middle of the table, they should be able to describe the fruits and the window in relationship to the globe and or the table. They should locate objects which are to the right and left of the globe as they face the scene.

Exercise 2-13, pg. 36. Read the students the following passage as a guided imagery. Then have them draw a picture of what you have described.
    Take a deep breath...hold it until I count to three...one, two, three...close your eyes and imagine that you are in a small area of the park.

you are sitting on a park bench...what is the park bench made of...what does
it look like....is it made of wood...or metal...or wood and metal...from where
you are sitting, there is a trash can on your left next to the park
bench...what color is it...what is it made of...is it large or small...what
shape is it....behind the bench are some trees...how tall are they...how
many trees are there...are all of the trees the same kind...are they
evergreen trees or leafy trees...now look to your right...there is a bed of
flowers...are they all the same kinds of flowers or are they different
kinds...what color are they....are they all the same color or are they
different....are they wild flowers....can you smell the flowers...if you can,
what do they smell like....take a moment and look around you again....look at
the trees....look at the flowers....look down at the park bench....look at the
trash can...on the count of three, open your eyes...one, two, three...open
your eyes.

Directions: In the space provided in the book, draw what you saw in the
guided imagery. Then do the exercises on pgs. 36 and 37.

In exercise 2-14 on page 38, either put the information on the blackboard and
have the students copy it, or if you have an advanced class, you may want to
use this as a listening exercise and have students locate and draw the objects
in the room according to your oral directions.
     When the students begin to write about the room, it's important for them
place themselves in the picture, so that they can use the phrases, "on my
right," "on my left," etc.

Exercise 2-15, pg. 40
     Answers to Checking Up
     1. Answers will vary.
     2. true

     Key Words and Phrases
     1. through 4. Answers will vary.

4

Chapter III - CLASSIFICATION

Skills: Sorting and grouping by similarities, labeling, making generalizations based on common qualities, using examples to support generalizations.

Pre-exercises (pgs. 44-46; exercises 3-A, 3-B, 3-C, 3-D)
These exercises give the students practice in recognizing common characteristics shared by a group. In pre-exercise 3-D on page 46, the students must devise the criteria for the classification. It is important that the students understand fully the concepts of labeling and classifying before they proceed further, as the entire chapter is based on this organizational principle.

Starting with Sentences (pgs. 47-51; exercises 3-1, 3-2, 3-3)
Exercises 3-1 and 3-2 on pages 47 and 48, add key works which are useful in making generalizations when writing a classification paragraph. Discuss the kinds of information which one might include in a paragraph introduced by one or more of the topic sentences in exercise 3-2 as preparation for future independent writing. Exercise 3-3 on pages 49-51 is best done as an in-class exercise to make sure that the students know the steps involved. Make sure that they understand the principle of listing and classifying items with shared qualities. You might also want to discuss with your class the notion that examples are used to represent a whole group and that the examples which they choose to use must support the topic sentence.

Building a Paragraph (pgs. 52-55; Guided Imagery and exercise 3-4)
Guided Imagery-Relax and sit back comfortably in your chair...relax your arms...relax your legs...take a deep breath...breathe out...take another deep breath and hold it...now breathe out and let your body be completely relaxed...imagine that there is a wedding in your family...you are celebrating the new marriage with your family and friends...look around you...listen to the sounds...now look at some of the people in the room...look at the women...what are they wearing...long dresses or short...are any of them wearing pants...what colors do you see...what fabrics are some of the clothes made of...can you see any jewelry...is it silver or gold...are the women wearing necklaces...rings...bracelets...earrings...are their heads bare or are they wearing hats...now look at the men...what are they wearing...are they wearing suits...are they wearing ties...what colors can you see...are there any children present...what are they wearing...are their clothes different from the clothes which the adults are wearing...are they brightly colored....now step back from the crowd and try to see them from far away...can you make a generalization about the clothing which the guests are wearing...is it fancy clothing...plain clothing...colorful clothing...formal clothing....informal clothing...now take a deep breath and when I count to three open your eyes...one..two..three.

Directions. Tell the students to make a generalization about the kinds of clothing they imagined that the guests at the wedding wore. It may be something like the following: The guests at the wedding all wore colorful clothing. In this case, every detail included in the paragraph would have to prove how colorful the clothing was. After they have decided what they want to say in the topic sentence, have them write a paragraph including examples of clothing from each group mentioned in the imagery.

In Exercise 3-4 on page 53-55, introduce the notion of consumer goods to the class by bringing in pictures and discussing the utility of items. Guide the discussion toward making the distinction between luxuries and necessities.

Make sure that members of the class choose representative examples for the three categories and that they explain <u>why</u> they did so. Use <u>relevant</u> and <u>specific</u> when discussing this exercise.

Exercise 3-5, pg. 56
    Answers to <u>Checking Up</u>
      1. classify   4. example
      2. label   5. kinds
      3. categories, variety

CHAPTER IV - DESCRIBING BY TELLING FUNCTION OF PARTS

<u>Skills</u>: Classifying, labeling, discarding, naming and locating parts, describing interrelationship of parts, identifying function of parts, grouping data according to function and transferring information from one form to another, describing relationship of parts to the whole.

<u>Pre-exercises</u> (pgs. 58-60; exercises 4-A, 4-B, 4-C)
As the students do these exercises, point out that labeling is a way of describing a whole group of items which are similar in function.

<u>Starting with Sentences</u> (pgs. 61-64; exercises 4-1, 4-2)
In these exercises it may be useful to draw items on the board and discuss the correct use of the vocabulary in naming sections, portions, layers, segments, and parts. Although you have probably already discussed the implied meaning of such words as <u>some</u>, <u>many</u>, <u>few</u>, and <u>several</u>, you might point out again that if you write <u>many</u> in a topic sentence, your reader expects to read about five or more items, examples, etc. You might also want to take one of the topic sentences and develop it into a paragraph on the board as an exercise in searching for relevant information.

<u>Building a Paragraph</u> (pgs. 65-81; exercises 4-3 through 4-9)
You may want the students to do exercise 4-3 on page 65, in class and assign exercise 4-4 on page 67 for homework.

Guided Imagery (pg. 69)
Take a deep breath and relax...etc....
Imagine that you are sitting at a table preparing to write...you pick up a pencil and look at it...is it a long pencil or a short one...what color is it...how many parts does it have...is the point sharp...press the point down on the paper...what mark does it leave...is there an erase on the end...how is the eraser attached to the pencil...what color is the eraser...what does it do...what is the longest part of the pencil made of...rub the pencil with your fingers...what does it feel like...rough or smooth...are there corners...is there any writing on the outside of the shaft of the pencil...what does it say...think of the number of parts that your pencil has...think of what each part does...what does each part look like...now take a deep breath and when I count to three, open your eyes...one...two...three.

<u>Directions</u>: The students may want to discuss the words which they will need to know in order to name the parts of the pencil.

In exercise 4-5 on pages 70 to 72, the students must transfer information from the first chart to the correct section of the second chart. You might want to point out that they will use the word <u>layer</u> when talking about the sections of the tree. The answers to the paragraph on pages 71 and 72 may vary slightly but should be as follows:

The leaves, <u>root hairs</u>, <u>roots</u>, <u>inner bark</u>, and <u>sapwood</u> provide.... The leaves are located <u>on the branches</u> and <u>manufacture food</u>.... The root hairs are located <u>on the roots</u> and absorb <u>water</u> and <u>minerals</u>. The <u>roots</u> are located underground and <u>carry</u> water.... The inner bark <u>is located between the cambium and the outer bark</u> and is a pathway for <u>food</u> to be carried.... The sapwood is located <u>between the cambium and the heartwood</u>. It also carries water. The outer bark is <u>next to the inner bark</u>.... The cambium layer, which is located next to the <u>sapwood</u>, allows the tree to <u>grow</u>. The roots and heartwood give...<u>tree</u>. The heartwood...<u>in the center</u>...<u>underground</u>.

In exercise 4-6 on page 73, the students should be reminded that facts in a paragraph should be listed in the same order that they appear in the topic sentence. You might also want to discuss the key words that signal changes in the topic within the paragraph. Exercises 4-7, 4-8, and 4-9 on pages 75 to 79, are similar in their method of approaching the material. If you have an advanced class, you may choose to have the students do only one or two of these exercises.

Answers to exercise 4-7, pg. 76

The different parts of an elephant have several functions. The tusks and the trunk are.... The tusks are used to scrape bark, dig out trees and dig for salt. The ears, the legs, the tusks, and the trunk are used for defense. The ears are used to frighten enemies. The legs are used to trample the enemy, and the tusk is used to attack the enemy. The trunk is used to locate an enemy. The body temperature...ears, which help to keep the animal cool. The trunk is used for communication. It is used for touching, stroking, and making sounds. Legs are used to support the animal's body.

Exercise 4-10, pg. 82
    Answers to Checking Up
A. 1. b.
   2. b.
   3. b.
   4. a.
B. Answers will vary.

CHAPTER V - EXPLAINING PROCESS

Skills: Extrapolating information, classifying and transferring information, recognizing and using chronological sequencing, giving and following directions, explaining operations in a process.

Pre-exercises (pgs. 85-90; exercises 5-A, 5-B, 5-C)
　　　These exercises require that the students be able to manipulate information so that it is listed in the correct order. If you feel that it is necessary, or if you have extra time, you may want to do an exercise in class in which you demonstrate something, and the students must tell the steps you went through in the correct order. A test of whether or not they have missed any steps will be to go back and do the demonstration again, following their directions this time. Suggestion: make a paper airplane in front of the of the class. Have them tell from start to finish the steps that you went throught. Put the steps on the board. Then have a student (or you) read the steps aloud and follow the directions exactly as they have been given. Make sure that the materials necessary for the procedure are mentioned before the demonstration.

Starting with Sentences (pgs. 91-96; exercises 5-1, 5-2, 5-3, 5-4)
You may want to spend some time discussing the vocabulary words in exercise 5-1 on page 92 so that students have time to ask questions about when the words are used. For instance, instructions and directions can be used interchangeably. With both of these words, we usually think of someone giving either written or spoken information that is precise. One would probably not use either of the words in a topic sentence inroducing a paragraph about everyday processes such as brushing your teeth or preparing breakfast unless, of course, you were emphasizing the precision required of the job. Steps and procedures refer to actually "doing" something. Chronology is implied in both of these words. Although they are often used interchangeably, procedures is a more formal word and suggests that a possibly more complicated explanation will follow. Things is the least formal and least specific of the of the words that might be used.
　　　Before starting exercise 5-2 on page 94, you may want to ask the students to choose words that they think might be appropriate in introducing the following:
　　　　making a paper airplane (steps, things, procedures)
　　　　putting together an unassembled toy (instructions, directions)
　　　　building a dollhouse, box, or some other non-commercially packaged item (steps, procedures, things)
　　　　cooking rice, spaghetti, baked potatoes, or some other common food (steps, things, procedures)
　　　　wiring a plug (procedures, steps, things, or possibly instructions or directions if you were using a snap-on variety of plug)
　　　　The answers to exercise 5-3 on page 95 are as follows:

1. 1	9. 7
2. 4	10. 14
3. 10	11. 3
4. 13	12. 8
5. 5	13. 11
6. 6	14. 12
7. 2	15. 15
8. 9	

Building a Paragraph (pgs. 97-101; exercises 5-5, 5-6)
Guided Imagery, (pg. 99)
　　　Sit comfortably in your chair and uncross your legs...close your eyes and

9

take a deep breath...exhale slowly...take another deep breath and hold it
while I count to three...one, two, three...now exhale slowly and concentrate
on my voice ..imagine that you are in a very small room...the room has no
windows...there is a door on one wall...the other walls are bare...look up at
the ceiling...it is very high...there is a small hole in the ceiling covered
by a piece of plastic...the only other thing in the room is a small bed...it
is six feet long and is covered with a mattress...now imagine that you have
locked yourself in this room by mistake...the door is too heavy to break...the
hole in the ceiling is too high for you to reach...there is no one around, so
you cannot call anyone to let you out...you must find a way to get out of the
room...think about how you will solve the problem...(long pause)...on the
count of three open your eyes, ready to write out your solution to the
problem...one...two...three.

Directions: On the paper in front of you write down your plan for escaping
from the room. Then tell what materials (items) you will need to help
you...write down each step of the process by which you will escape. When you
have finished making your notes, write a topic sentence that will tell your
reader where you were (the room) and how you escaped. Use the past tense.
It might be helpful to draw a picture of the room first.

Exercise 5-7, pg. 102
    Answers to <u>Checking Up</u>
    A. 1. descriptive   6. function
       2. function   7. descriptive
       3. process   8. function
       4. descriptive
       5. process
    B. Answers will vary.

CHAPTER VI - COMPARING AND CONTRASTING

<u>Skills</u>: Sorting qualities, classifying, clarifying generalizations with details, abstracting specifics from generalizations, understanding key words in topic sentences, using key words in topic sentences.

<u>Pre-exercises</u> (pgs. 104-105; exercises 6-A, 6-B): After the students have completed the exercises above, you might bring in two real items - an electric can opener and a manually operated can opener, for instance, and discuss the similarities and differences between the two. Have the students brainstorm and put their responses on the blackboard. Then have them try to label the ways in which the items are similar and the ways in which they are different. Some categories may be as follows: function, color, size, shape, operation. They should be able to do pre-exercise 6-C on page 106 independently.

<u>Starting with Sentences</u> (pgs. 107-111; exercises 6-1 - 6-7): Extra practice with the abstract words which are commonly used in comparison or contrast paragraphs may be useful if there is time or if the students have particular difficulty. In exercise 6-1 on page 107, point out that the phrase <u>approximately the same</u> changes to <u>approximately the same as</u> depending on the word order and usage in the sentence, e.g. Joan's weight is <u>approximately the same as</u> John's. Joan is <u>approximately the same</u> size as John. Joan and John are <u>approximately the same</u> size. It will also be useful to discuss the noun form of the verb <u>generalize</u>.
    In exercises 6-2 and 6-3 on pages 109 and 110, the students must give the concrete information from the charts to support the generalizations. Discussing the use of <u>both</u>, <u>however</u>, and <u>but</u> as key words which help to express similarity or difference should be useful to them when they begin writing independently.
    Before doing exercise 6-3, we found that group discussion of similarities and differences between the tiger and the cat (both belong to cat family; one is wild, one is tame) and the dog and wolf (both belong to canine family; one is wild, one is tame) was helpful. Before doing exercise 6-5 (A and B) on page 113, try to bring in large pictures of fruits, animals, etc. so that the class can discuss as a group the similarities and differences between items in the same group before they actually work independently. For example, a picture of a green squash and a yellow squash might be compared. A hamburger might be contrasted with a sandwich; a Cadillac with a Mercedes; a seagull with a chicken; a butterfly with a moth. As final preparation, the class might do a group paragraph on the differences between men and women. This kind of brainstorming as a group prior to independent writing allows the students to practice articulating their ideas and to question which forms are best to use in expressing their thoughts. Another suggestion for class discussion might be have the class think of two kinds of vegetables which are similar (carrots and potatoes, for instance). Then ask them to write down the ways in which they are similar (both grow underground, both are hard, both have a pitted outer skin, both have leafy parts which appear above the surface of the ground.
    Note: There is an opportunity in the class discussions to use <u>because</u> in responses. Since they will be using this kind of a response in later chapters, it might be a good idea to introduce it here.
    In Exercise 6-6 on page 114, the students are asked to make a distinction between sentences which suggest that two items can be compared or contrasted and sentences which are factual and need no explanation or proof. If they have difficulty getting started with this exercise, you might have them underline the words in the sentences which give them clues, e.g. In sentence one, the words <u>all</u>, <u>some</u>, and <u>characteristics</u> suggest that more information

will be forthcoming.

Answers - Exercise 6-7, page 115.
A. 2,1,3,4,6,5,7
B. Key Words
similarities and differences, climate, SW and SE.
In both areas, conditions are similar
both
In contrast, winter, in southwestern region, spring
both, southeastern
alike in some ways, different in others
Students who are good readers will have no difficulty in finding the key
words, but many students have not learned to look for the words in reading and
should benefit from articulating the reasons for their choices.

Guided Imagery - page 116.
Before doing the guided imagery, you may want to tell the story about the
six blind men and the elephant. The first man touched the elephant's side.
it was rough and extended as far as he could reach in any direction; he
thought it must be a wall. The second man touched the trunk of the elephant.
It was long and cylindrical; he thought it must be a snake. The third man
touched the tail. It was long and round and hard and had sharp bristles on
it; he thought it must be a rope. The fourth man touched the elephant's ear.
It was flat and smooth and shaped like a triangle; he thought it must be
a fan. The fifth man touched the elephant's leg. It was round and thick and
hard; he thought it must be a tree trunk. The sixth man touched the
elephant's tusk. It was smooth and hard and pointed on one end; he thought
it must be a spear.
Discuss the conclusions which the men drew based on the knowledge which
they had. You might want to do a class exercise in which students try to
describe something in the classroom (or something you bring into class)
without naming it, e.g. The object I'm thinking of is rectangular; it is
about one-half the size of the door (window). The object I'm thinking of is
hard and rectangular and flat. It is supported by four rectangular pieces of
wood, one at each corner (desk). Encourage them to use comparison and/or
contrast in their clues, e.g. The object is hard like the door, but it is not
as large (window).

Now do the guided imagery which follows:

Relax and breathe deeply...when I count to three, take a deep breath and
hold it ...one, two, three...now release the breath and feel your body
relax...think of an object which you are familiar with...imagine that it is in
front of you...how large is the object...is it very large...very small...is it
the size of anything else that you know well...feel the object...is it
rough...smooth...pitted...can you compare the texture to anything else that
you know...pick up the object...is it heavy...is it light...is it the same
weight as anything else you can think of...what shape is the object...does it
feel round...square...rectangular...triangular...is it flat or three
dimensional...does the object make a sound...what does it sound like...what
other things about the object are interesting or unusual...now prepare
yourself to come back...take a deep breath and release it and open
your eyes....

Directions: Now, write about the object which you have imagined. You
will be describing as many things about it as you think will help the reader
to know what it is, but you should not name the object. If you wish, you may
begin your paragraph by completing the following sentence: "The object which
I'm thinking of is..."

When the students have finished writing, they may exchange their books with each other and try to guess what object their partners have written about.

Exercises 6-8 through 6-14; pages 117-136.
These exercises give the students practice in extrapolating information from charts and pictures and using the information in building paragraphs which compare and/or contrast. We have omitted the answers here as they seem self-explanatory. Prior to doing Exercise 6-12 on page 130, however, an in-class exercise might be inserted to check on the general level of competency in comparison/contrast. A suggestion might be to have the students compare/contrast the way they are today with the way they were five years ago. You might have them jot notes down in two columns on a sheet of paper; they might then write a short comparison or tell the class how they feel that they have changed (or not changed) in five years. This kind of an exercise provides a nice break from the ones in the workbook because the students can use their own personal experiences.

Exercise 6-15, page 137-138.
    Answers to Checking Up
    1. a.   7. similarity
    2. b.   8. differences
    3. a.   9. steps
    4. c.   10. things
    5. similarities   11. parts
    6. differences   12. through 22. Answers will vary.

CHAPTER VII - USING EXAMPLES TO SUPPORT OR EXPLAIN

<u>Skills:</u> identifying examples; thinking of relevant examples; giving enough relevant details; narrating an incident; writing a topic sentence; giving multiple examples to support a topic; finding concrete specifics to illustrate abstractions.

<u>Pre-exercises</u> (pgs. 141-143; exercises 7-A, 7-B, 7-C)
Prior to beginning the pre-exercises, you might have the students watch a short segment of "silent TV" (almost any situation comedy or soap opera will do. "Three's Company" provides some good, broad facial expressions and pretty clearcut emotions. After they have watched a short segment, they can discuss what emotions they think the actors were expressing. If the class is advanced, you might want to have them writer short dialogues to match the emotions.
    The purpose of the pre-exercises is to get the students to think in terms of specific and sufficient detail to support generalizations.

<u>Starting with Sentences</u> (pgs. 144-146; exercise 7-1, 7-2)
    Before the students begin working on the exercises individually, you may want to have the class brainstorm a sentence in class so that they have an idea of using an incident or example to support a topic sentence. One possibility might be as follows:
    "Some English expressions are so unclear that I have difficulty understanding them."
    Have the students tell you about expressions that they have heard but have not understood. Write the expressions of the board (you might want to cluster the expressions as you go along). The students might discuss what they think the expressions mean and compare their impressions with the real meaning in our culture. This is a place where you could include some information about writing a paragraph containing examples, e.g. If you're giving short examples, try to have at least three in order to support your topic sentence convincingly. If you're using an elongated example or incident, be sure to include enough details to make the reader understand culture. This is a place where you could include some information about what happened. Answering the questions <u>who</u>, <u>what</u>, <u>where</u>, <u>when</u>, and <u>why</u> will often provide the kinds of details which are necessary.

<u>Building a Paragraph</u> (pgs. 146-152; exercises 7-3, 7-4, 7-5)
    On pages 146 and 147, two examples are given. If students are still having difficulty thinking of concrete incidents to prove the sayings, here are three more sayings which can be used in class to promote discussion.
    "A rolling stone gathers no moss."
    "Too many cooks spoil the broth."
    "Many hands make light work."
    Exercises 7-4 on page 149 and 7-5 on page 150 have been set up so that the student can use what he "knows" personally to develop the paragraph. He/she should be encouraged to elaborate by giving details for each example. Brainstorming reactions to emotions, e.g. what kinds of things to you <u>do</u> to express anger, happiness, or grief. A brief guided imagery like the one below may also help to generate specific details about behavior.

    Guided Imagery - Relax and take a deep breath. Breath in and our slowly...now take a deep breath....hold it...now release the air from your lungs...feel yourself getting more and more relaxed...now, think of a time when you were very angry...what caused you to feel angry...try to remember how your body felt when you were angry...how did you feel inside...how did your stomach feel...did you breath more quickly...did you feel hot or cold....now concetnrate on the outside of your body...on your hands...your

legs...your face...could you feel your muscles tightening up...did your facial
expressions change...what happened to the outside of your body....concentrate
on what you said ....what was your voice like...what did you say exactly...did
you call someone a name...did you say nothing at all...did you feel like
saying something but were afraid...did you make any noise....was it loud or
soft...try to remember how other people have acted when they have been
angry...what did they do...what did they say...what did they look like...now
take all of the images which you have and on the count of three, open your
eyes...one, two, three...open your eyes.

After the students have completed the guided imagery, have them discuss the
reactions which they remembered from when they were angry or when they
observed another person being angry. Have them apply the same kind of details
to writing about feelings of grief in exercise 7-4 on page 149.

GUIDED IMAGERY (pg. 152)

Relax, uncross your legs, etc. Take several deep breaths...now take a breath
and hold it while I count three...one, two, three...Imagine that you re
standing on a playground in a park...there are many children on the
playground...they are all doing things which make them happy...they are all
having fun...look around you...see the equipment on the play area...are there
any swings...slides...climbing bars...now look at the children...what are they
doing...what expressions do you see on their faces...what sounds do you
hear...are they loud...are they soft...are people talking...are people
laughing...what does the laughter sound like...what does the talking sound
like...is it loud...is it soft...is it fast...is it slow...concentrate on the
children who are having fun...listen to them carefully...watch them
carefully...what are they doing...what are they saying...what sounds are them
making...Now prepare yourself to come back to the room...remember the
expressions on the individual faces...remember the sounds and actions which
showed happiness and joy...on the count of three, you will return to the
room...one, two,three.

Directions: Write the word happiness on a piece of paper. Then write down
all of the different ways expressions of happiness which you imagined in the
guided imagery...Use this topic sentence for your paragraph - "Children on the
playground express their happiness in various ways." Write the sentence on
the board, or if the class is advanced, let them come up with their own topic
sentences. Now write a paragraph supporting the topic sentence by giving as
many examples (describing actions and sounds) as you can. You must give at
least three examples.

Students may want to read their papers aloud, or you may want them to work
in groups, reading their papers to each other. Since we anticipate that one
of the structural problems here will be the use of key words, this might be a
good place to have the students view the papers on an overhead projector and
correct together in class.

Exercise 7-6, pg. 153.
    Answers to Checking Up
    1. c
    2. b
    3. b
    4. b
    5. c

CHAPTER VIII - USING REASONS TO SUPPORT YOUR OPINION

Skills: Making a judgment based on facts or observation; expressing an opinion; expressing reasons for the opinion; giving explanations or examples to support reasons, odering information for emphasis.

Pre-exercises (pgs. 157-159; exercises 8-A, 8-B)
The three parts of exercise 8-A on pages 157 and 158 require that the students make decisions based on information which is concrete and given. NOTE: In exercise 8-A, number 2, the money figure in plan 2 should be $200 not $300. Exercise 8-B on page 159 requires that the student discover a simple relationship between the given items.
      You may want to do some classroom brainstorming to provide further practice in expressing reasons fully. Suggestions for topics for classroom brainstorming and clustering might be as follows:
      Television is/is not essential to our daily lives.
      Women should/should not work outside of the home.
      Men should/should not help with the household chores.
Try to have the students identify the issue first, and to express it in a question. The question for the first topic might be as follows:
      What does television provide for us?
By listing all of the things which television provides (e.g. entertainment, information, etc.) first, the student can determine whether or not television is essential to daily life and form his opinion based on what he has listed.
      Another possibility for pre-exercises in class might be to divide the class into groups and have the students quickly react to a list of topics by giving an opinion and a reason. Possible topics might include the following: ice cream, doing dishes, soccer, women's/men's fashions,dogs.
      e.g. I like ice cream because it's nutritious.
You may extend the exercise so that the students must also give an explanation for their reasons.

Starting with Sentences (pgs. 159-165; exercises 8-1, 8-2, 8-3, 8-4, 8-5)
These exercises give the students practice in recognizing and using key words and phrases which are common to reason paragraphs; ordering information and the key words which may be used to connect bits of information are also stressed.

Building a Paragraph
Answers - exercise 8-6, page 166.
A. 1. reason   2. reason   3. example   4.example   5. example   6. reason
7. example   8. example   9. example
B. Answers will vary. I prefer to live in a warm climate for three reasons.
C. Answers will vary.
D. Answers will vary.

Guided Imagery (pg. 175)
Take a deep breath...now exhale...take another deep breath and hold it till the count of three...one...two...three...take another deep breath and let it out slowly...breath in...breath out...imagine that you are at home in your living room...you are watching television when the doorbell rings...you get up to answer the door...when you open the door, you see a person whom you have known in the past...this is a person whom you once loved and trusted as your best friend...who is this person...now imagine that this person did something in the past which was against you...what did he do...did he steal from you...was he mean to you...this person now asks you for help...he needs money...his child is sick, and he must buy medicine to make him well...you have money, but you remember what this person did to you...he begs you for money now...how do you feel about this person...do you want to lend him the

money...do you want to shake his hand or embrace him...do you want to slam the door in his face...what do you want to say to him...imagine how you feel and what you want to do and say...(long pause)...on the count of three, open your eyes...one, two, three...

<u>Directions</u>: On a piece of paper, write down your decision about lending the person money. Then write down the reasons why you would or would not do it.

Before the students actually write the paragraph, have some of them present their decision and reasons to the class. When a sufficient amount of discussion has taken place, they should write a paragraph (or two if you wish) explaining the situation and their decision. They should write a topic sentence which briefly explains the situation to the reader - tell who the person is and explain what he wants. Tell them to write a sentence which explains the past situation - what the person did - and to state whether or not they will lend the person the money. Ask them to give their reasons and remind them to give explanations to support the reasons.

Exercise 8-10, pg. 176
    Answers to <u>Checking Up</u>

A paragraph developed by reason will include an opinion, reasons to support the opinion, examples or explanations to support the reasons, and a concluding sentence which summarizes.

The concluding sentence summarizes the main reasons for the opinion. Usually this means that the writer refers to the main reasons. (see pg. 164)

I might include a phrase such as <u>in my opinion</u>, or <u>I think</u> or <u>believe</u> at the beginning of the sentence.

I need an explanation or example after every sentence in order to prove my point to my reader. If I don't give concrete information, there is no reason for my reader to accept my opinion as being true.

PRENTICE-HALL, ENGLEWOOD CLIFFS, NEW JERSEY 07632

0-13-918251-9